Evidence-Based Instruction in Reading

A Professional Development Guide to Vocabulary

Evangeline Newton

The University of Akron

Nancy D. Padak

Kent State University

Timothy V. Rasinski

Kent State University

PEARSON

Boston • New York • San Francisco
Mexico City • Montreal • Toronto • London • Madrid • Munich • Paris
Hong Kong • Singapore • Tokyo • Cape Town • Sydney

Executive Editor: *Aurora Martínez Ramos*
Series Editorial Assistant: *Lynda Giles*
Marketing Manager: *Danae April*
Production Editor: *Gregory Erb*
Editorial Production Service: *Publishers' Design and Production Services, Inc.*
Composition Buyer: *Linda Cox*
Manufacturing Buyer: *Linda Morris*
Electronic Composition: *Publishers' Design and Production Services, Inc.*
Cover Designer: *Kristina Mose-Libon*

For related titles and support materials, visit our online catalog at
www.ablongman.com.

Between the time website information is gathered and then published, it is not
unusual for some sites to have closed. Also, the transcription of URLs can result in
typographical errors. The publisher would appreciate notification where these
errors occur so that they may be corrected in subsequent editions.

Library of Congress Cataloging-in-Publication Data
Newton, Evangeline.
   Evidence-based instruction in reading : a professional development guide
to vocabulary / Evangeline Newton, Nancy D. Padak, and Timothy V. Rasinski.
      p.   cm.
   Includes bibliographical references and index.
   ISBN-13: 978-0-205-45631-4 (alk. paper)
   ISBN-10: 0-205-45631-6 (alk. paper)
   1. Vocabulary--Study and teaching (Elementary) 2. English
language--Orthography and spelling--Study and teaching (Elementary) I. Padak,
Nancy. II. Rasinski, Timothy V. III. Title.
   LB1574.5.N48 2008
   372.61--dc22   2007026118

Printed in the United States of America

10 9 8 7 6 5 4 3 2 1   RRD-VA   11 10 09 08 07

All photos appear courtesy of the authors.

Among us, we have been teachers and teacher educators for nearly 100 years! During this time, we have developed deep and abiding respect for teachers and trust in their ability to offer their students the very best possible instruction. Yet we also agree with librarian John Cotton Dana (1856–1929), who said, "Who dares to teach must never cease to learn."

Our careers have been marked by continual learning. We dedicate this book to all who have taught us and all whom we have taught—all who have dared to teach.

NP
TR
MM
EN
BZ

About the Authors

Evangeline Newton is Professor of Literacy Education and Director of the Center for Literacy at the University of Akron. She teaches literacy methods courses and professional development workshops to elementary and middle school teachers in Ohio school districts. She also chairs the Reading Review Board of the Ohio Resource Center for Mathematics, Science and Reading. Dr. Newton has researched and written on several topics. With Tim Rasinski, Nancy Padak, and Rick M. Newton, she coauthored *Building Vocabulary from Word Roots (Levels 3–8)*, a curriculum series for elementary and middle school students. She serves on the Editorial Review Board of *The Reading Teacher* and was a co-editor of *The Ohio Reading Teacher*. A former St. Louis public school teacher, she holds a BA degree from Washington University in St. Louis, an MAT degree from Webster University, and a PhD from Kent State University.

Nancy D. Padak is a Distinguished Professor of Education at Kent State University where she directs the Reading and Writing Center and teaches graduate courses in literacy education and recently received the honor of Kent State University Distinguished Professor. She was a part of the team that wrote the initial grant to fund the state literacy resource center at Kent State University–Ohio Literacy Resource Center (OLRC) and has been a middle school and high school classroom teacher and administrator in a large urban school district. She frequently works with teachers and has written or edited a dozen books and more than 100 scholarly articles. Professor Padak is a past College Reading Association President and a former editor of *The Reading Teacher*. She currently edits the *Journal of Literacy Research*.

Timothy V. Rasinski is a Professor of Education in the Department of Teaching, Leadership, and Curriculum Studies at Kent State University. He teaches graduate and undergraduate courses in literacy education. His major interests include working with children who find reading difficult, phonics and reading fluency instruction, and teacher development in literacy education. He has published over 100 articles and 10 books on various aspects of reading education. Dr. Rasinski is past editor of *The Reading Teacher* and is currently an editor for the *Journal of Literacy Research*. He has served as president of the College Reading Association and on the Board of Directors of the International Reading Association. He earned bachelor's degrees in economics and education at the University of Akron and the University of Nebraska at Omaha. His master's degree in special education also comes from the University of Nebraska at Omaha. Dr. Rasinski was awarded the PhD from The Ohio State University.

Contents

Series Introduction

Evidence-Based Instruction in Reading: A Professional Development Guide

Better than a thousand days of diligent study is one day spent with a great teacher.

JAPANESE PROVERB

*L*earning to read is perhaps a young child's greatest school accomplishment. Of course, reading is the foundation for success in all other school subjects. Reading is critical to a person's own intellectual development, later economic success, and the pleasure that is to be found in life.

Similarly, teaching a child to read is one of the greatest accomplishments a teacher can ever hope for. And yet, reading and teaching reading are incredibly complex activities. The reading process involves elements of a person's psychological, physical, linguistic, cognitive, emotional, and social world. Teaching reading, of course, involves all these and more. Teachers must orchestrate the individuality of each child they encounter; the physical layout of the classroom and attendant materials; their own colleagues, parents, and school administration; the school's specified curriculum; and their own style of teaching! The popular cliché that "teaching reading is not rocket science" perhaps underestimates the enormity of the task of teaching children to read.

The complexity of teaching reading can be, quite simply, overwhelming. How does a teacher teach and find mastery of the various skills in reading, attending to the school and state curricular guidelines, using an appropriate variety of materials, while simultaneously meeting the individual needs of all children in the classroom? We think that it was because of the enormous complexity of this task that many teachers resorted to prepackaged reading programs to provide the structure and sequence for a given grade level. Basal reading programs, for example, provide some assurance that at least some of the key skills and content for reading are covered within a given period of time.

The problem with prepackaged programs is that they are not sensitive to the culture of the classroom, school, and community; the individual children in the classroom; and the instructional style of the teacher. The one-size-fits-all approach adopted by such programs—with, of course, the best of intentions—resulted in programs that met the minimal needs of the students, that lacked the creative flair that only a teacher can give a program, and that absolved teachers of a good deal of the accountability for teaching their students. If children failed to learn to read, it was the fault of the program.

The fact of the matter is that many children failed to learn to read up to expectations using prepackaged programs. The results of periodic assessments of U.S. students' reading achievement, most notably the National Assessment of Educational Progress, have demonstrated little, if any, growth in student reading achievement over the past 30 years. This lack of growth in literacy achievement is at least partially responsible for equally dismal results in student growth in other subject areas that depend highly on a student's ability to read.

The National Reading Panel Report

Having noticed this disturbing trend, the National Reading Panel (NRP) was formed by the United States Congress in 1996 and given the mandate of reviewing the scientific research related to reading and determining those areas that science has shown have the greatest promise for improving reading achievement in the elementary grades. In 2000, the NRP came out with its findings. Essentially, the panel found that the existing scientific research points to five particular areas of reading that have the greatest promise of increasing reading achievement: phonemic awareness, phonics and word decoding, reading fluency, vocabulary, and reading comprehension. Additionally, the NRP indicated that investments in teachers, through professional development activities, hold promise of improving student reading achievement.

The findings of the NRP have been the source of considerable controversy, yet they have been used by the federal and state governments, as well as local school systems, to define and mandate reading instruction. In particular, the federal Reading First program has mandated that any school receiving funds from Reading First must embed within its reading curriculum direct and systematic teaching of phonemic awareness, phonics, reading fluency, vocabulary, and comprehension. The intent of the mandate, of course, is to provide students with the instruction that is based on best evidence that it will have a positive impact on students' reading achievement.

Although we may argue about certain aspects of the findings of the National Reading Panel, in particular what it left out of its report of effective instructional principles, we find ourselves in solid agreement with the panel that the five elements that it identified are indeed critical to success in learning to read.

Phonemic awareness is crucial to early reading development. Students must develop an ability to think about the sounds of language and to manipulate those sounds in various ways—to blend sounds, to segment words into sounds, and so on. An inability to deal with language sounds in this way will set the stage for difficulty in phonics and word decoding. To sound out a word, which is essentially what phonics requires of students, readers must have adequate phonemic awareness. Yet, some estimates indicate that as many as 20 percent of young children in the United States do not have sufficient phonemic awareness to profit fully from phonics instruction.

Phonics, or the ability to decode written words in text, is clearly essential for reading. Students who are unable to accurately decode at least 90 percent of the words they encounter while reading will have difficulty gaining appropriate meaning from what they read. We prefer to expand the notion of phonics to word decoding. Phonics, or using the sound–symbol relationship between letters and words, is, without doubt, an important way to solve unknown words. However, there are other methods to decode written words. These include attending to the prefixes, suffixes, and base elements of longer words; examining words for rimes (word families) and other letter patterns; using meaningful context to determine unknown words; dividing longer words into smaller parts through syllabication; and making words part of one's sight vocabulary, words recognized instantly and by sight. Good readers are able to employ all of these strategies and more. Appropriately, instruction needs to be aimed at helping students develop proficiency in learning to decode words using multiple strategies.

Reading fluency refers to the ability to read words quickly, as well as accurately, and with appropriate phrasing and expression. Fluent readers are able to decode words so effortlessly that they can direct their cognitive resources away from the low-level decoding task and to the more important meaning-making or comprehension part of reading. For a long time, fluency was a relatively neglected area of the reading curriculum. In recent years, however, educators have realized that although fluency deals with the ability to efficiently and effortlessly decode words, it is also critical to good reading comprehension and needs to be part of any effective reading curriculum.

Word and concept meaning is the realm of *vocabulary*. Not only must readers be able to decode or sound out words but they must also know what these words mean. Instruction aimed at expanding students' repertoire of word meanings and deepening their understanding of already known words is essential to reading success. Thus, vocabulary instruction is an integral part of an effective instructional program in reading.

Accurate and fluent decoding of words, coupled with knowledge of word meanings, may seem to ensure *comprehension*. However, there is more to it than that. Good readers also actively engage in constructing meaning, beyond individual words, from what they read. That is, they engage in meaning-constructing strategies while they read. These include ensuring that they employ their background knowledge for the topics they encounter in reading. It also means that they ask questions, make predictions, and create mental images while they read. Additionally, readers monitor their reading comprehension and know when to stop and check things out when things begin to go awry—that is, when readers become aware that they are not making adequate sense out of what they are reading. These are just some of the comprehension strategies and processes good readers use while they read to ensure that they understand written texts. These same strategies must be introduced and taught to students in an effective reading instruction program.

Phonemic awareness, phonics/decoding, reading fluency, vocabulary, and comprehension are the five essential elements of effective reading programs identified by the National Reading Panel. We strongly agree with the findings of the NRP—these elements must be taught to students in their reading program.

Rather than get into in-depth detail on research and theory related to these topics, our intent in this series is to provide you with a collection of simple, practical, and relatively easy-to-implement instructional strategies, proven through research and actual practice, for

xii
....
SERIES
INTRODUCTION

*Evidence-Based
Instruction in
Reading*

teaching each of the five essential components. We think you will find the books in this series readable and practical. Our hope is that you will use these books as a set of handbooks for developing more effective and engaging reading instruction for all your students.

Professional Development in Literacy

Effective literacy instruction requires teachers to be knowledgeable, informed professionals capable of assessing student needs and responding to those needs with an assortment of instructional strategies. Whether you are new to the field or a classroom veteran, ongoing professional development is imperative. Professional development influences instructional practices which, in turn, affect student achievement (Wenglinsky, 2000). Effective professional development is not simply an isolated program or activity; rather it is an ongoing, consistent learning effort where links between theoretical knowledge and the application of that knowledge to daily classroom practices are forged in consistent and meaningful ways (Renyi, 1998).

Researchers have noted several characteristics of effective professional development: It must be grounded in research-based practices; it must be collaborative, allowing teachers ample opportunities to share knowledge, as well as teaching and learning challenges, among colleagues; and it must actively engage teachers in assessing, observing, and responding to the learning and development of their students (Darling-Hammond & McLaughlin, 1995). This professional development series, *Evidence-Based Instruction in Reading: A Professional Development Guide* is intended to provide a roadmap for systematic, participatory professional development initiatives.

Using the Books

The *Evidence-Based Instruction in Reading* series consists of five professional development books, each addressing one major component of literacy instruction identified by the National Reading Panel (2000) and widely accepted in the field as necessary for effective literacy programs: phonemic awareness, phonics, vocabulary, fluency, and comprehension. These five components are not, by any means, the only components needed for effective literacy instruction. Access to appropriate reading materials, productive home–school connections, and a desire to learn to read and write are also critical pieces of the literacy puzzle. It is our hope, however, that by focusing in-depth on each of the five major literacy components, we can provide educators and professional development facilitators with concrete guidelines and suggestions for enhancing literacy instruction. Our hope is that teachers who read, reflect, and act on the information in these books will be more able to provide effective instruction in each of the five essential areas of reading.

Each book is intended to be used by professional development facilitators, be they administrators, literacy coaches, reading specialists, and/or classroom teachers, and program participants as they engage in professional development initiatives or in-service programs within schools or school districts. The use of the series can be adapted to meet the specific needs and goals of a group of educators. For example, a school may choose to hold a series of professional development sessions on each of the five major components of literacy instruction; it may choose to focus in depth on one or two components that are most relevant to their literacy program; or it may choose to focus on specific aspects, such as assessment or instructional strategies, of one or more of the five areas.

The books may also be useful in professional book club settings. An icon, included at spots for book club discussion, marks times when you might wish to share decisions about your own classroom to get colleagues' feedback. You might also want to discuss issues or solve problems with colleagues. Appendix B lists several other possible book club activities. These are listed by chapter and offer opportunities to delve into issues mentioned in the chapters in greater depth. It is important that, in collaboration with teachers, professional development needs be carefully assessed so that the appropriate content can be selected to meet those needs.

Overview of Book Content

To begin each book in the series, Chapter 1 presents a literature review that defines the literacy component to be addressed in that book, explains why this component is important in the context of a complete and balanced literacy program, and synthesizes key research findings that underlie the recommendations for evidence-based instructional practices that follow in subsequent chapters. The conclusion of Chapter 1 invites professional development program participants to analyze, clarify, extend, and discuss the material presented in this chapter.

xiii
....
SERIES
INTRODUCTION
*Evidence-Based
Instruction in
Reading*

xiv

SERIES
INTRODUCTION

*Evidence-Based
Instruction in
Reading*

Chapter 2 outlines general principles for instruction. Participants are asked to evaluate their own instructional practices and to plan for refinement of those practices based on their students' needs. Each suggested instructional strategy in this chapter is based on the research presented in Chapter 1 and includes the purpose, necessary materials, and procedures for implementation. Ideas for engaging professional development participants in extended discussions related to phonemic awareness, phonics, vocabulary, fluency, or comprehension are offered at the end of Chapter 2.

Chapter 3 begins by presenting broad themes for effective assessment such as focusing on critical information, looking for patterns of behavior, recognizing developmental progressions, deciding how much assessment information is needed, using instructional situations for assessment purposes, using assessment information to guide instruction, and sharing assessment information with children and families. At the end of Chapter 3, professional development participants are asked to evaluate their current assessment practices, draw conclusions about needed change, and develop plans for change.

Key issues related to teaching English language learners (ELLs) are presented in Chapter 4. The chapter also invites participants to think beyond classroom-based strategies by examining activities that can be recommended to families to support children's development of phonemic awareness, phonics, vocabulary, fluency, and comprehension at home. The final chapter provides a variety of print- and Web-based resources to support instruction in phonemic awareness, phonics, vocabulary, fluency, or comprehension.

Together, the information and activities included in these books, whether used as is or selectively, will foster careful consideration of research-based practice. Professional development participants will learn about the research that supports their current practices and will be guided to identify areas for improvement in their classroom programs.

The need for new programs and methods for teaching reading is questionable. What is without question is the need for great teachers of reading—teachers who are effective, inspiring, and knowledgeable about children and reading. This series of books is our attempt to guide teachers into a deeper understanding of their craft and art—to help already good teachers become the great teachers that we need.

Introduction

Vocabulary

*T*hink back to your own early literacy school experiences. How did you learn to read? What kinds of instructional activities do you recall from your elementary classrooms? Which experiences made learning to read enjoyable? Were there any that you found to be difficult or mundane? What was the role of vocabulary in your own instruction as a child? What was it like to learn new words in school?

Chances are that "word study" was a big part of how you learned to read. Yet, other than memorizing the definitions of new or "key" words and writing them in a sentence, most teachers have difficulty recalling vocabulary activities that were part of their own school routines. Typically, teachers remember learning how to sound out words and how to spell them accurately. Given that vocabulary is the foundation of all oral and written communication in school, it is puzzling that most of us can recall very few activities around exploring word *meanings.*

Everyone agrees that an extensive vocabulary helps us share our thoughts and feelings more effectively with others. Not surprisingly, an extensive vocabulary is also central to reading comprehension. The more words a reader is familiar with, the easier it is for him or her to understand the meaning of a text (National Reading Panel, 2000). The last few decades have seen considerable research attention devoted to vocabulary instruction, although few of the findings have managed to influence classroom practice. One reason for this may lie in the complex nature of words themselves: What does it really mean to "know" a word? In this book, we explore this question and what it means for classroom instruction.

Before delving into the material that follows about research on vocabulary, instructional strategies, assessment, and resources, we recommend that you examine your current understanding, beliefs, and possible misconceptions about vocabulary instruction. The following multiple-choice questions can serve as a starting point to activate background knowledge on this topic:

1. _____ The smallest unit of meaning in language is a
   a. morpheme
   b. grapheme
   c. phoneme
   d. letter

2. _____ A word's meaning depends largely on the
   a. context in which it is used
   b. part of speech
   c. reader's interpretation
   d. phonetic rules

3. _____ Words can have
   a. the same sounds but different meanings
   b. different sounds but the same spelling
   c. the same spelling but different meanings
   d. all of the above

4. _____ "Passive" vocabulary refers to
   a. nouns and pronouns
   b. words we are indifferent to
   c. words we recognize but don't know well
   d. words we don't recognize at all

5. _____ "Active" vocabulary refers to
   a. verbs
   b. words we use regularly
   c. words we can say but not define
   d. words we recognize

6. _____ According to the *Oxford English Dictionary,* how many meanings are there for the word *run?*
   a. 82
   b. 43
   c. 6
   d. 28

7. _____ One of the best ways to expand vocabulary is through

    a. wide reading
    b. spelling lists
    c. writing compositions
    d. memorization

8. _____ Learning a new word "concept" requires

    a. 5 exposures
    b. 12 exposures
    c. multiple exposures
    d. multiple exposures in different contexts

9. _____ Which of the following is a good way to teach vocabulary?

    a. student exploration of various resources
    b. word sorts
    c. direct instruction of key words
    d. wide reading
    e. all of the above

10. _____ Which of the following is *not* a good way to teach vocabulary?

    a. memorizing definitions
    b. direct instruction of key words
    c. word games (Wordo)
    d. literature discussions

(The answer key is at the end of this section.)

How did you do on this brief pretest? Whether you did well or struggled with some of the questions, we hope that this quiz helps you see that vocabulary instruction is a complex issue. It involves learning *new words for familiar concepts,* as well as learning *new concepts for familiar words.* And it involves learning and applying a unique set of strategies to unlock those meanings.

The good news is that once they have mastered a few investigative techniques, most students enjoy the process of unlocking and exploring word meanings. We hope that this professional development tool will clarify and enhance your knowledge of the nature of word meanings, and the role that vocabulary plays in literacy instruction. With strategies for how to teach and assess your students' vocabulary knowledge, you can support students in their "word adventures."

Book Club

As you prepare to begin this professional development program, we invite you to consider and discuss with colleagues the following items that may help frame your interpretation and application of the material in this book. Take some time now to write notes about these aspects of your literacy program, particularly with regard to vocabulary instruction:

- Describe the conditions under which you work.

  _____

  _____

  _____

  _____

- Describe the major goals of your literacy program.

  _____

  _____

  _____

  _____

- What are the principles that ground, or serve as a rationale for, your program?

  _____

  _____

  _____

  _____

- Describe your daily schedule or classroom routine, particularly as it relates to vocabulary instruction.

  _____

  _____

  _____

  _____

- Describe the materials that you currently use for vocabulary instruction.

  _____

  _____

  _____

  _____

- How are parents involved in your literacy program?

  _____

  _____

  _____

  _____

- How do you currently assess student progress in vocabulary growth?

  _____

  _____

  _____

  _____

The chapters that follow are intended to provide an organizational framework for vocabulary instruction that will assist you in identifying elements that are effective and offering suggestions when modifications need to be made. Chapter 1 presents an overview of current research and professional literature on vocabulary instruction. Research-based answers are provided for questions such as what vocabulary is, why vocabulary instruction is important, and how instruction can be most effective. The end of the chapter invites you to analyze, clarify, extend, discuss, and apply information learned from this chapter.

Chapter 2 focuses on research-based instructional practices. General principles for early literacy instruction in vocabulary are presented first. Then, you are asked to use a semantic feature analysis to evaluate your own instructional practices, considering both instructional practices that are effective and those in need of fine-tuning. The strategy suggestions that follow include ideas that can form the backbone of your vocabulary instruction.

Chapter 3 focuses on assessment and begins by describing broad truisms of assessment that can be applied to all aspects of literacy learning. After working with these broad assessment ideas, you are asked to examine more closely your own current assessment practices in terms of both critical elements of vocabulary and how you assess individual students. Graphic organizers are provided for goal planning, reflection, and curriculum alignment.

Chapter 4 addresses vocabulary instruction for ELLs and moves beyond classroom-based strategies and considers recommendations for families to use at home to support their children's vocabulary development. Parents' frequently asked questions about vocabulary are also addressed in this chapter.

Chapter 5 provides instructional and professional resources for teaching vocabulary. Throughout the book you will find ample room to make notes about various aspects of planning and implementing effective vocabulary instruction. We encourage you to use these spaces to record insights and ideas that are particularly pertinent to your own instruction. Doing so should provide you with the kind of concrete plan of action you'll need to offer students more consistent and effective opportunities to develop their vocabularies.

Answer Key: 1–a; 2–a; 3–d; 4–c; 5–b; 6–a; 7–a; 8–d; 9–e; 10–a

Vocabulary Instruction: What Does Research Tell Us?

2
....

CHAPTER 1

*Vocabulary
Instruction:
What Does
Research Tell Us?*

*K*amil and Hiebert (2005) write that vocabulary is a bridge between the "word-level processes of phonics and the cognitive processes of comprehension" (p. 4). This is a useful way to visualize the importance of vocabulary for young readers. The National Reading Panel (2000) states that if a word is not in a child's oral vocabulary, reading comprehension is hindered. Just as we teach children strategies for identifying or decoding the *sounds* of unfamiliar words, we must also teach them strategies for analyzing and exploring the *meanings* of unfamiliar words.

Until recently, most formal vocabulary instruction has been limited to the introduction of key words before reading a new text. Yet, the National Reading Panel (2000) found that vocabulary is learned both indirectly and directly and that dependence on only one instructional method does not result in optimal vocabulary growth. We must do more. In this section, we define the concept of vocabulary and highlight important evidence-based research findings that clarify its critical role in reading comprehension instruction.

What Is Vocabulary?

It may surprise you to know that the word *vocabulary*, like most English words, has an interesting history. In ancient Rome, schoolchildren were required to learn lists of new words—in Latin, of course—by saying them out loud with their voices (*voc-*). They demonstrated "proficiency" by reciting these vocabulary lists to their teachers. Our English word, *vocabulary*, then, is built on the Latin word for "voice," and literally means an "oral list of words." Even as adults, Romans continued the habit of reading everything out loud. Roman doctors would often order sick patients to give up reading for awhile because reading would irritate their vocal cords and make a sore throat worse! And did you know that the words *vowel* and *vocabulary* share the same Latin base: *voc-*. That's because we need our voices to say *a, e, i, o, u* (Rasinski, Padak, Newton, & Newton, 2007).

Although the words we use have interesting histories, words themselves are constructed from tiny units of sound (phonemes) that form units of meaning (morphemes). We use letters and letter patterns (graphemes) to spell or represent those meanings in print. But very often there is no simple one-to-one connection between the sound (or spelling) of a word and its meaning. Consider these examples:

- Define the word *running* in each of these sentences:

  I am *running* in a marathon.

  My neighbor is *running* for city council.

  My refrigerator is *running* in the kitchen.

As you now know, the *Oxford English Dictionary* gives 82 different definitions for the word *run*! Happily, all share a core meaning of "movement," but each use of *running* also has a unique meaning because of its sentence context. Sometimes, then, the study of vocabulary involves learning new concepts for familiar words.

- Now, explain what the words *bear* and *bare* mean in each of these sentences:

  Hiking through the forest, John and Mary grew afraid of the *bears*. They could not *bear* the cold and blowing snow, so they looked for shelter to protect their *bare* hands and faces. Finding a *bare* room, Mary asked John to *bear* with her as she built a fire. They shared a *bear-hug* to stay warm while they waited for the fire to heat the room.

In this case, although "bears" in a forest and "bearing" the cold share the same spelling, they do not share the same core meaning. Some words have the same spelling but different meanings. Similarly, although "bears" in a forest and "bare" hands share the same sounds, their meanings are entirely different. Some words have the same sounds but different spellings and meanings. Sometimes the study of vocabulary involves learning different concepts for words that look or sound alike.

So, simply put, vocabulary instruction is the fascinating study of word meanings. English word meanings are especially interesting because they have come to us from many different cultures, both ancient and modern. Like America itself, word meanings are complex, diverse, and always changing as the world we live in changes.

Why Is Vocabulary Important?

Unfortunately, students who begin school with smaller vocabularies find themselves at an academic disadvantage that most of them never overcome (Hart & Risley, 1995). It only makes sense: Young readers

4
....

CHAPTER 1

*Vocabulary
Instruction:
What Does
Research Tell Us?*

who lack adequate vocabulary knowledge cannot apply word recognition strategies efficiently. Baffled, they become frustrated and are quickly left behind by those readers who do have adequate word knowledge. The result is an escalating cycle of reading failure for too many children. In fact, decades of research has consistently found a deep connection between vocabulary knowledge, reading comprehension, and academic success (Baumann & Kameenui, 2004).

Beginning readers must grasp that the fundamental purpose of reading is to comprehend or "make meaning." Early reading instruction has focused much of its attention on the phonological aspect of word learning, so it's easy to forget that many children do not automatically understand what the words mean once they have decoded them. For them, learning to read new words often means learning to understand new concepts or new labels for familiar concepts. Although a child may successfully decode a word, meaning will not automatically follow if the concept that word represents is not already part of his or her experiential vocabulary. That's why a solid bank of conceptual knowledge is especially important for beginning readers. By bringing meaning to the sounds of a word, wide conceptual knowledge assists the strategy of decoding.

A wide vocabulary is especially important for success in school beyond early reading. As students move from grade to grade, literacy tasks become more complex. Most researchers believe that children naturally add between 2,000 to 3,000 new words each year to their vocabularies, and by the fifth grade they meet 10,000 new words in their reading alone (Nagy & Anderson, 1984). The sheer number is daunting!

In addition, many of these words represent concepts in the content areas of math, science, or social studies. Children need to understand the concept of "photosynthesis," for example, before they can internalize and apply its word label. Complicating matters even further, the same word may appear in more than one content area and represent a unique concept in each. A "revolution" in history is quite different from the "revolution" of the earth around the sun. Instruction that builds children's conceptual knowledge through word exploration and systematic attention to word analysis will help students read fluently and comprehend and discuss what they have read. Most important, it will show students that discovering the rich variety of meanings—often in a single word—is an appealing pursuit.

How Do I Support Vocabulary Growth?

The first steps in planning a vocabulary component for your reading program involve looking at your current practices:

- Do you currently tuck vocabulary discussion into all lessons?
- What word analysis strategies do you teach?
- How do you choose words for direct instruction?
- What do you do to stimulate word curiosity?
- Do your students have additional opportunities within each school day for "word play" with others?
- Do your students have opportunities to explore words independently, particularly with electronic and print resources?
- How often do you share words you find interesting?

Keep these questions in mind as you read the following important principles for vocabulary instruction. Later in the book we will give you specific strategies in each of these areas.

Read to Your Students Every Day

Listening to stories is one of the great joys of childhood. Since a child's listening vocabulary is about two years ahead of his or her reading vocabulary (Biemiller, 2001), daily read-alouds can introduce children to words and concepts that they may not yet be ready to read independently. To expand students' conceptual and content knowledge, your read-alouds should include a wide range of textual materials, both fiction and nonfiction. As they listen to high-quality literature, students meet vivid new words through engaging stories shared in a supportive setting.

Consider this example: You have decided to read Eric Carle's *Walter the Baker*, which describes how the pretzel was "invented." As children listen to you read, they visualize a town *encircled* by a wall. They learn that a baker who makes *tarts* may be *banished* from the *Duchy* unless he invents a *tasty* roll, one through which the sun can shine. The words *encircled* and *banished* may be new concepts but are easy to grasp in the context of the story. Similarly, children can easily figure out that a *tart* must be a kind of sweet because Walter bakes

6
....

CHAPTER 1

*Vocabulary
Instruction:
What Does
Research Tell Us?*

"pies, cookies, cakes, and tarts." And what about a *Duchy?* Well, they may realize it refers to a place, but might need to meet it a few more times before they "own" it.

Listening to stories is one of the best ways to expand vocabulary because a word's general meaning is always "cued" by the semantic, structural, and oral contexts in which it is encountered. Each time the same word appears in a text or conversation, a child's understanding of it will deepen, even without looking the word up in the dictionary. Best of all, as children experience new worlds through the high-quality language of children's literature, their vocabulary expands in a way that is natural and pleasurable.

Tuck Vocabulary Instruction into All Lessons, Both Directly and Indirectly

Direct word learning is planned. It includes both teacher-initiated discussion and student-initiated personal investigation. The National Reading Panel (2000) found that although some direct instruction of key words is useful, it should not be the only teaching method. Research indicates only about 8 to 10 new words can be learned each week through direct instruction (Stahl & Fairbanks, 1986). Moreover, students will not master new words unless they have frequent opportunities to meet them again.

Indirect word learning is therefore essential. It comes from using oral language in conversations that explore ideas or share experiences. Such conversations deepen the understanding of familiar concepts and broaden the awareness of new ones. They also give children practice in seeing and hearing the same words in a variety of contexts.

Using instructional methods that combine direct and indirect word learning is easier than you might think. Consider this example: You have decided to read *Koala Lou*, Mem Fox's delightful tale about a koala bear who trains for the "Bush Olympics," to your first-grade class. You think that the concept of a koala bear will be new to your students, so you have planned to teach it through direct instruction. You begin by asking students to tell what they know about bears in general. Then you show them a picture of a koala and ask how it is similar and how it is different from bears they already know. You may write some of these observations on the board to revisit in discussion.

Before reading, you invite students to take a "picture walk" through the text and ask them to raise questions or make comments.

You might ask them to predict some of the words they might expect to meet in this book. You write some of those words on the board. Next, your students look at the pictures as they listen. As you read, students may interject observations or raise questions. One student, for example, may comment that the "Bush Olympics" is a lot like our Olympics. Another may assert confidently that her mother, like Koala Lou's mother, also loves her and "always will." Perhaps someone will raise a question about koalas and how they live.

When you have finished, you ask students to describe their favorite part of the story. You revisit their prereading observations about koala bears and ask if they have anything to add. You revisit the words they had predicted and see how many were actually in the book. You might end the lesson by asking whether they would like to know more about koala bears and encourage students to find more information in other books or on the Internet.

Your reading of *Koala Lou*, then, involved both direct and indirect word learning that drew on students' thinking, listening, and discussion skills. The result was new conceptual knowledge and vocabulary growth that was easily embedded in a lesson that also gave students rich language experience.

Teach the Word Analysis Strategies of Context Clues and Word Roots

Context clues and word roots (morphology) are two strategies that are particularly important for vocabulary development. *Context clues* is probably the most frequently used reading strategy for determining the meaning of an unknown word. Although context in reading has many dimensions, it most often refers to figuring out the meaning of an unknown word by getting help from the words, phrases, sentences, or illustrations surrounding it (Harris & Hodges, 1995). That help may be semantic, based on the meaning of the preceding or following passages. It may also be structural, based on grammatical markers within a word or sentence.

Using context clues is an especially important strategy for vocabulary development because, as we noted earlier, many English words have multiple meanings. Identifying which meaning is the best fit depends entirely on the context in which it is being used. Consider this example: "The bandage was *wound* around the *wound*." In its first appearance, *wound* is a verb that describes an action; in the

8
....

CHAPTER 1

*Vocabulary
Instruction:
What Does
Research Tell Us?*

second, it is a noun that describes an injury. The word has the same spelling in both spots but entirely different meanings (and pronunciations). Try saying the sentence again with the noun *wound* first and then the verb *wound*. Did you notice that the sentence makes no sense? Only the semantic and structural contexts can deliver the correct meaning!

Context has an important role in oral language as well. Think about the many English expressions that people use on a daily basis. What does it mean to be the "apple" of someone's "eye," or announce that you have "an axe to grind" with someone? Although most of us understand and take such colorful expressions for granted, they can be confusing to young children, particularly those for whom English is a second language. But if the observation that a baby is the "apple of her mother's eye" is delivered with a smile and in a gentle voice, the meaning of the phrase becomes clear. Context in oral language, then, can include ways we use our voice and bodies to reinforce our meaning. Learning how to use the surrounding semantic context—whether grammatical, structural, or oral—helps children expand vocabulary.

Word Roots. We always teach young children about "word families," letter patterns that generate a common sound and spelling (*cake, bake, take, rake*). We also teach them about affixes (prefixes, suffixes). But we sometimes neglect to emphasize that these are "word roots" that generate the same meaning in many different words. By separating and analyzing the meaning of a prefix, suffix, or other word root, children can often unlock the meaning of an unknown word. If we teach students that the prefix *tri-* means "three," for example, they can use that information to figure out *tricycle, trio,* and *triplets.* When introducing the concept of "photosynthesis," we can easily point out its roots: *photo* means "light" and *syn-* means "with." As children grapple with the complex process of how light (*photo-*) is combined with (*syn-*) carbon dioxide and water to make sugar, knowledge of these word roots will support their efforts.

Knowing that words can be broken down into meaning units is a powerful strategy for vocabulary development. Until recently, teaching word roots was a strategy reserved for upper-grade or content area classrooms. But a growing body of research tells us that this strategy should be introduced early. In fact, by the second grade, students should be adept at using word roots as a vocabulary strategy (Biemiller, 2005). (In the next chapter, we will talk about how to teach word roots through the strategy of "Divide and Conquer" [Newton & Newton, 2005].)

Provide Time for Students to Read Independently and to Talk about What They Have Read

Wide reading and frequent discussion provide multiple opportunities to use new vocabulary in different contexts. Moreover, a well-respected line of research has clearly established that in order to expand their vocabularies, students need to read extensively (Blachowicz & Fisher, 2000). It only makes sense: The more children read, the more they meet the same words in both familiar and new contexts.

Much of the reading children do in school is necessarily focused on specific skill instruction. The texts they read usually represent their developmental levels. But the school day should also include opportunities for children to choose texts of high interest to them, even those that are too easy or too difficult. Even a simple text can generate conversation that will expand students' conceptual knowledge and increase their overall word awareness. Similarly, children should also be allowed to revisit familiar texts. After all, don't we enjoy watching movies we love again and again? Each time we see them we spot something new. And have you ever waded through a difficult or confusing article because the topic was important to you? If so, you probably stuck with the article long enough to satisfy your curiosity, and in the process you learned something new. Even with the youngest children, provide time for library visits to choose books for independent reading.

Talking about what you have read not only expands a child's vocabulary but it also enhances his or her communication skills. In fact, talking with others is essential to vocabulary development. Describing a story's character or events gives children an opportunity to use new vocabulary in an oral context. Explaining information they have read about a topic to others deepens a child's new conceptual knowledge. Furthermore, answering peer questions through discussion—or asking questions of others—gives a child practice in using words and concepts for real-world communication. Even with the youngest children, provide time for sharing independent reading through book talks or literature circles (Daniels, 2002).

Create a Classroom Setting That Stimulates Word Curiosity and Word Exploration

As noted earlier, research tells us that we learn more new words incidentally than we do through direct instruction (Lehr, Osborn, &

Hiebert, 2004). Encourage playful activities where students can investigate words or solve word puzzles by themselves or in the company of others. Help students learn how to explore dictionaries as well as other print and electronic resources for word learning. Make sure your classroom provides children with easy access to information about words and regular opportunities to display or use what they are discovering. The goal is *word awareness.*

If you are teaching a unit about families, for example, create a chart with the alphabet. Ask students to think of words for each letter that describe a family. Write the words under each letter: They may not think of any words for *a*, but *b* might have *brother*, or *baby*, or *beautiful. C* might have *cat*, or *cool.* Remember that discussion builds vocabulary, so make sure to ask them how each word they think of connects to "family." Post the chart and ask students to keep thinking about family-related words for any letters not filled in. As a word comes to mind, you or they can fill in the letter: *A* is for *always*, because families are "always there for us."

You might also post a "Root-of-the-Week" on chart paper and invite students to search for other words that share the roots. The prefix *re-*, for example, is found in many words that children use every day. If a dictionary is handy, you will find students checking it out for new *re-* words to add.

Giving students time to do crossword puzzles and word scrambles or to create riddles and tongue twisters is not only fun, it's good instruction! Make time for students to play and explore word games on their own or with others. "Wordo" (a version of the familiar "Bingo") is a great way to reinforce new vocabulary. And don't forget that all children love to perform! "Word Theater" is a vocabulary version of the popular game "Charades." Have students choose a word from that alphabet chart and act out its meaning, while others try to guess which word is being presented. Older students can even develop short skits that dramatize a new word. Imagine how many ways *cool* might be presented!

The Internet may be a teacher's best friend when it comes to word exploration. There are countless easily accessible—and free— word activities available for students to do on the Internet (see Chapter 5). Electronic dictionaries are particularly good because they are visually pleasing, with hypertext links to more information. At WordCentral.com, students can build their own dictionaries! And remember that short history of the word *vocabulary?* Students will enjoy investigating lots of word histories on their own by checking out "Word-of-the-Day" sites designed with young learners in mind. Other Internet resources provide word games (puzzles, scrambles, memory,

Hangman) and activities with word roots. You may want to put a few key sites on the desktop of your classroom computers. Playing with these electronic resources can become a "learning center" or free-time activity.

While encouraging your students to explore words, don't forget to share your own love of words as well. Each of us has favorite texts that we turn to because the words move us to laughter or tears. Read these aloud to your students, and talk about the power of words in your own life.

It will take your students an entire lifetime to explore the vast array of words people use. Your most important vocabulary teaching goal, therefore, is to provide students with the tools they will need to start on a lifelong adventure of word exploration. Celebrate the joy of words by reading to them and allowing them to read on their own. Immerse them in high-quality words through planned instruction and spontaneous teachable moments. Show them how to unlock the meaning of unfamiliar words through the use of context and analysis of word roots. Help students discover the pleasure of pursuing new words on their own.

Don't concentrate all your efforts on teaching a limited number of words. Keep the focus on word awareness and on the word analysis skills your students will need to determine meaning. In addition, focus on increasing opportunities for students to use words, some familiar and some new, in a variety of settings and contexts. Finally, as you think about vocabulary, always keep the definition of vocabulary presented at the beginning of this section in mind as you work with students: Vocabulary is the fascinating study of word meanings.

Professional Development Suggestions

ACED: Analysis, Clarification, Extension, Discussion

I. REFLECTION (10 to 15 minutes)

ANALYSIS:

- What, for you, were the most interesting and/or important ideas in the vocabulary introduction and literature review presentation?

_____

_____

_____

_____

- What information was new to you?

_____

_____

_____

_____

CLARIFICATION:

- Did anything surprise you? Confuse you?

_____

_____

_____

_____

EXTENSION:

- What questions do you have?

_____

_____

_____

_____

II. DISCUSSION (20 minutes)

- Form groups of 4 to 6 members.
- Appoint a *facilitator (timer)* and *recorder.*
- Share responses. Make sure that each person has shared his or her responses to each category (Analysis/Clarification/Extension).
- Help each other with any areas of confusion.
- Answer and/or discuss questions raised by group members.
- On chart paper, the recorder should summarize the main discussion points and identify issues or questions the group would like to raise for general discussion.

III. APPLICATION (10 minutes)

- Based on your reflection and discussion, how might you apply what you have learned from the vocabulary introduction and literature review?

_____

_____

_____

_____

CHAPTER 2

Instructional Strategies for Vocabulary Development

After years of teaching kindergarten and primary grades, Ms. Santos expects a wide range of developmental levels and literacy foundations among her young students. Some children enter school from literacy-rich home environments where they have been immersed in language. Some have had lives filled with books that parents, grandparents, caregivers, or siblings read to them often. Some have had a wide range of community or travel experiences, with abundant opportunities to engage in conversation with others. These children will probably have large vocabularies, with adequate conceptual knowledge to support their school instruction. They will understand, for example, what a fairy tale is or why a wolf is dangerous.

Others arrive in the classroom from homes where literacy has not been emphasized. They have heard few books, had few community or travel experiences, and had little opportunity to engage in conversation with others. In addition, a growing number of kindergarten and primary-level children have native languages other than English. Even though they may come from homes with rich language experiences, they have limited knowledge of English vocabulary. For all these reasons, Ms. Santos knows that in order to support vocabulary development for all her students, she needs to differentiate her instructional plans.

Furthermore, Ms. Santos understands that like adults, children have two kinds of vocabularies. There are words they make use of *actively*, generating them easily as they write and speak. But there are also words children make use of *passively*. These are words children recognize when they hear or read them, but they are not part of their daily lexicon. Since many of the words children meet in school fit this latter category, Ms. Santos knows that classroom activities should support children's vocabulary development in both ways. Given these facts, she makes certain that her instructional routines reflect three important principles:

- Children need *daily* instruction, both direct and indirect, focused on the study of word *meanings.*
- Children need *strategies* for unlocking word meanings, and time to practice them.
- Children need to develop *word awareness* by exploring new words on their own and in the company of others. It may surprise you to know that just five minutes of word play each day

can build a child's vocabulary and improve reading comprehension. (Rasinski & Padak, 2004)

Having these principles firmly in mind, then, facilitates the development of instruction.

Professional Development Suggestions

Book Club

Evaluating Your Own Instruction

Before adding new strategies and activities to your instructional repertoire, it is important to evaluate your current teaching practices: What
current vocabulary instructional practices do you find to be effective?
What areas need to be fine-tuned? Are there instructional components
that are not being covered to the degree that they need to be?

To help you in evaluating your current instructional practices,
consider the semantic feature analysis chart on the next page. Along
the side of the chart, you will see space for you to list those instructional strategies that you currently use to enhance children's vocabulary development. Across the top of the chart, you will see
components that may be present in the activities that you listed. Of
course, not every component can, or should, be part of every activity.
Some activities will encourage students to interact with classmates, for
example; others may invite a more independent response. The key is
to seek a balance in terms of the variety of strategies used so that a
range of developmental levels and diverse learner needs can be effectively addressed.

Take the time to complete the semantic feature analysis. Place
a + sign in the corresponding box for each attribute that is present in
a vocabulary instructional activity that you currently use. More than
one attribute may be present for each activity that you list. You may
wish to collaborate with colleagues, as doing so helps individuals to
recall the additional vocabulary strategies that they use during the
course of the school year.

When the semantic feature analysis is complete, it should help
you see which aspects of vocabulary instruction currently receive a
great deal of attention in your classroom and which aspects may not
currently receive enough emphasis. Knowing this will help you to better plan adjustments in your instructional routine. Discuss your findings and insights will colleagues.

Semantic Feature Analysis for Current Vocabulary Instructional Practices

Vocabulary Strategies	Key Words	New Concepts	Word Analysis Strategies	Word Exploration and Play	Oral Language Practice	Written Language Practice

Strategy Suggestions

The vocabulary development instructional strategies described in this section have all been found effective through research. They are divided into three areas: (1) strategies for building or deepening conceptual knowledge; (2) strategies for word analysis; and (3) strategies for word exploration and play. In general, each can be adapted to work successfully with children in grades K–3 (and beyond). In the descriptions we indicate common procedures and materials, but you should feel free to innovate!

Building Conceptual Knowledge

Each word we use represents a concept. This means that all vocabulary instruction is based on building or deepening students' conceptual knowledge. Before children can truly learn a new word, however, they must already understand the concept it represents. When introducing new vocabulary, then, it is essential that children have adequate background or prior knowledge about the topic being read. Even if your students already have sufficient background knowledge of the topic, you will need to help them connect that knowledge with the new concepts and/or new word labels they will be meeting.

Remember that research tells us the number of new words children can learn each week through direct instruction is quite small (Stahl & Fairbanks, 1986). For this reason, select words for direct instruction carefully. Beck, McKeown, and Kucan (2002) suggest you choose words that (1) represent a significant concept for a topic of study, (2) are needed for a specific reading assignment, and, perhaps most important, (3) are likely to be encountered in other texts.

In the following strategies you will notice that students themselves volunteer many of the words for study. Through the use of prediction, categorization, and discussion, they make connections that help them build new conceptual knowledge. As you use these strategies with your students, make sure you tuck in a few words that you want them to learn as well!

Word Predictions

This strategy from Hoyt (1999) may be used with a text you are reading to children or with one they are reading in a small or whole

20
....

CHAPTER 2

*Instructional
Strategies for
Vocabulary
Development*

group. Once they become familiar with the procedure, your students can do this activity independently or with a partner.

Purpose:

To focus on vocabulary as a way to activate background knowledge and support reading comprehension.

Materials:

A reading selection, either fiction or nonfiction. Students will need some prior knowledge of the topic under study.

Procedures:

1. Read the title and ask students, based on the title, what they think the selection may be about.
2. Next, invite them to walk through the text with you, just looking at the pictures.
3. Now, using the pictures and the title of the book as clues, ask students to predict what words they think may be in the selection. Tell them you are interested only in "juicy" words that might tell about the characters or meaning of the story.
4. As students call out words, write them on chart paper. Before writing each word, make sure to ask students why they chose it. You can make this list as long or short as you choose, but 6 to 10 words is adequate.
5. When your list is complete, either read the story to students or ask them to read it to themselves. Tell them to watch and see if the words on the list appear in the text. (If the selection is long, you may want to stop once or twice and visit the list.)
6. After you have read the text, have a brief discussion about the text. Did students enjoy it? What were their favorite parts?
7. Now go back and revisit the words they predicted. Put a check next to any words that were in the text. Return to the list and discuss where and how the words were used. Ask students to speculate about why the other words might not have appeared in the reading. You might ask if there are any other "juicy" words that should be added.

At this point, you have a nice list of words that can be used for a variety of extension activities. The chart can be displayed and used in an assortment of activities that ask students to categorize, act out, retell, or write (see List-Group-Label and Word Theater later in this chapter).

Vocab-o-Gram

This strategy, also known as Prevoke, may be used with a text you are reading to children or one they are reading to themselves. It may be used as a whole-group, small-group, partner, or individual activity.

Purpose:

To "sort" words from a reading selection into categories by predicting where they will be encountered. This strategy can be used to introduce key vocabulary, develop classification skills, demonstrate that words have multiple potential meanings, and support comprehension.

Materials:

A reading selection, either fiction or nonfiction, chart paper, and/or an individual sheet of paper with three or four columns for each student. (Students may also fold a piece of paper into three columns or four boxes.)

Procedures:

1. Decide on 6 to 10 key words that are important in the text to be read. If using fiction, identify words that would fit each of these categories: setting, characters, problem, and solution. Adapt the categories to fit your needs. For younger children, for example, you may want to use "people," "places," and "things that happen." If using nonfiction, adjust the categories to fit the content.

2. Write the words on the board or on chart paper. Ask the students to share what they know about the meaning of each word. If they do not know a word, tell them the meaning.

3. Once you are sure students have a basic understanding of each word, write the categories on the board. Review the categories and then tell the students that each word belongs to one of these categories.

4. Ask the students if they can predict which words belong in which category. You may guide this discussion as a whole-group

activity, or invite students to work together in pairs. Either way, remind them that some of the words may fit more than one category, so whenever they put a word into a column they need to explain why they think it belongs there.

5. When word placement discussion has ended, ask a few students to predict what the text will be about. You may want to write those predictions on the board. Ask students if any questions were raised by their discussion. If so, write a few of these as well.

6. Next, read the selection to students, or ask them to read it silently.

7. After reading, have a brief discussion about the story. Did the students enjoy it? What were their favorite parts?

8. Then revisit the predictions students made. Where were they accurate? Ask students to review the categories. How did they do? Identify the correct categories, but make sure to discuss why other choices were possible.

At this point, you have a nice list of words that can be used for a variety of extension activities. The chart can be displayed and used in an assortment of activities that ask students to categorize, act out, retell, or write (see List-Group-Label, Word Theater, and Word Skit later in this chapter).

Story Impressions

This strategy, adapted from Blachowicz and Fisher (2006), may be used with a text you are reading to children or with a text they are reading in a small or large group. It can also be done as a writing activity. Once they become familiar with the procedure, students can do this independently or with a partner.

Purpose:

To provide "hands-on" practice with new vocabulary and deepen conceptual knowledge through use of the same words in different contexts.

Materials:

A fictional text or a list of 5 to 10 words that give the "impression" of setting, character trait, action, and feelings.

Procedures:

1. List (and number) the words in the order in which they appear in the story. If these are not words from a story, list them in an order that resembles the order of a story.

2. Review each word so that the students have at least a general understanding of its meaning.

3. Now ask the students to write a story, using the words in that order. If these are words from a story, tell them to write the story as they might if they were the author. Depending on time constraints, you may want to tell the students to do a five-minute "quickwrite," or limit their story to one paragraph. Students may work independently or write with a partner. For younger students, you may want to use the Language Experience Approach (Rasinski & Padak, 2004) here: Ask the group to write a story together. With your guidance, they dictate as you write their story on a sheet of large chart paper.

4. When the stories are finished, ask the students to read them orally. You may want to do this as a "read-around," where students jump in and read their selections without others commenting until all stories have been read. Tell the students to listen for ways in which their stories are similar and different. If you have written a story together, read it chorally and ask the children to think about how many different kinds of stories they could have written with those words.

5. Now read the author's selection, or go directly to a general discussion comparing the stories students generated.

6. Return to the vocabulary and highlight different ways in which the words were used. Clarify any confusion about what the words mean.

Authors and Illustrators

This activity from Rasinski, Padak, Newton, and Newton (2007) is a variation of "Story Impressions" that works well for many students as a partner activity. In this version, students work with a partner to write a story. You provide 5 to 10 words on the board, but this time the children may use the words in any order they want. Once they have finished their stories, partners trade stories with another partner team. Each team reads the new story and draws a picture to illustrate some part of the story. Students then share illustrations, explaining what they drew and why they chose that part. The discussion about their illustrations is a good way to practice new vocabulary.

List-Group-Label

This all-purpose categorization strategy may be used as a before- or after-reading activity. It also works well when used to activate background knowledge and/or review material on a topic of study. It may be used as a whole-group, small-group, partner, or individual activity.

Purpose:

To brainstorm vocabulary words related to a topic. It can be used to activate background knowledge, review content, develop classification skills, and demonstrate that words have multiple meanings.

Materials:

Chart paper and/or an individual sheet of paper for each student. A reading selection, either fiction or nonfiction, is optional.

Procedures:

1. Ask the students to brainstorm all the words they can think of on a topic. List the words on the chalkboard or on chart paper so that everyone can see them. You can also add a few words you want them to consider.

2. Ask the students for a quick explanation of the meaning of each word on the list. Make sure unfamiliar words have been explained.

3. Now, working as a whole group or in teams, ask the students to organize the words into categories of two words or more. Tell them to develop their categories by finding words from the list that share common characteristics. Explain that they will need a label that describes the characteristic for each category, and that all words must be used.

4. Ask the students to volunteer the categories they have developed. If working as a whole group, write the categories and words on the board. Point out that some of the words fit more than one category, so whenever they put a word into a column they need to explain why they think it belongs there.

5. If the students are working in small teams, have each team share with the entire class. Make sure the students explain how they

came up with their categories. As they analyze words and concepts in small- or whole-group discussion, they will better understand the concepts each word represents, and how words can have multiple meanings.

At this point, you have one or more lists of words and categories that can be used for a variety of extension activities. If used as a before-reading activity, students can return to the categories and see whether they reflect the content of the reading. If not, how did they differ? The chart of categories can also be displayed for future activities as well.

Word Theater

This versatile strategy (Hoyt, 1999), based on the popular game Charades, uses pantomime and oral language to make word meanings concrete for young children. It can be used in a variety of ways, including before or after reading a text selection. It can also be tucked into spare moments or when children need a stretch. It works especially well as a partner or small-group activity.

Purpose:

To build or reinforce conceptual knowledge by acting out the meaning of a new or familiar vocabulary word.

Materials:

A list of at least ten words that can be dramatized easily. The list may be taken from a topic under study or a reading selection. You might also have students brainstorm a list of words they find interesting.

Procedures:

1. List the words on the chalkboard or on chart paper so that everyone can see them. Tell students that they will select one word and then work with a partner to act out its meaning, but without speaking.
2. Ask the students to find a partner. Each child should read the list of words to his or her partner. When both partners have read the list to each other, they should choose a word. Tell them they have two minutes to decide how to get the word's meaning across by acting it out.

3. Now ask each team to act out its word while the other students try to guess which word they have chosen. Make sure the list of words is visible, so that the students can keep reading and rereading the words as they try to figure out which one is being pantomimed. As they look for connections between the acting and the word list, they will better understand the concepts each word represents.

Word Skits

This strategy (Rasinski, Padak, Newton, & Newton, 2007) is an "advanced" version of Word Theater that works well with students who are both experienced in pantomiming words and comfortable working in small teams of three or four. Each team chooses one word and writes its definition on an index card. Working together, they create a skit or situation that shows the meaning of the word. The skit is performed without words. Classmates try to guess the word being shown. Once the word is correctly identified, the definition is read out loud.

Using Root Word Analysis and Context

Discovering that certain letter patterns or "word families" regularly generate the same sound is an important word analysis skill children learn in phonics instruction. When *ake* appears in *cake, rake,* and *snake,* for example, it is always pronounced the same way. But it is just as important for children to discover that certain letter patterns regularly generate the same meaning. When the prefix *re-* appears in *return, replace,* and *refund,* for example, it always means "back." In fact, over 60 percent of the new words students encounter will have word parts that always carry the same meaning (Nagy et al., 1989).

In addition to looking for word families, then, children must also learn how to look for meaning in a word's "root" parts. This means teaching students how to look for roots and/or familiar words when trying to figure out the meaning of an unfamiliar word. By separating and analyzing semantic patterns, students can often figure out a word's meaning or build new words on their own.

Root is a generic or "umbrella" term for any word part that holds meaning (Ayers, 1986). There are three kinds of roots: prefixes, bases, and suffixes. A *prefix* is a root placed at the beginning of a word (e.g., *re*do, *in*vention). A *base* is a root that provides a word's main meaning. It can be a whole word (pre*pay*) or a word part (e.g., pre*dict*). A *suffix* is a root placed at the end of a word (e.g., color*ful*, color*less*). Suffixes sometimes indicate parts of speech (happ*ily* is an adverb; happ*iness* is a noun) or verb tense (e.g., jump*ed*, jump*ing*).

Teaching the meaning of prefixes is especially helpful to young children because a few prefixes are used in a large number of words. Moreover, nine prefixes account for 75% of the words that use prefixes (White, Sowell, & Yanagihara, 1989). Furthermore, prefixes always mean the same thing and are spelled the same way, no matter where they appear. See Appendix A for a list of roots that often appear in words used at the primary and upper elementary level. Many children will already be familiar with some of the words that use these roots. Because of this, they will quickly grasp the meaning and enjoy discovering other word that use the same root. You may even want to introduce one of these roots every Monday as a "Root of the Week" (described later in this chapter).

Every teacher knows that learning how to use context clues to predict the meaning of an unknown word is one of the most important comprehension strategies we can teach beginning readers. Explicitly connecting the use of context clues to vocabulary learning will help students grasp that a word's conceptual meaning is directly linked to the situation in which it is being used. Predicting what a new word might mean based on the passages that surround it is not always automatic for young children, so occasionally using activities that reinforce context clues will promote metacognitive growth.

The following strategies develop word analysis skills that will help students automatically apply their knowledge of word roots and context to figure out new vocabulary.

Divide and Conquer

Whenever they encounter unknown words, students can use this strategy (Rasinski, Padak, Newton, & Newton, 2007) to identify semantic units and build a "connection" that unlocks a word's meaning. You may introduce and practice this routine with familiar compound words or prefixes. Once students become comfortable with the procedure, they can apply it as they explore new words in a variety of learning contexts.

Purpose:

To help students understand that words are often made up of recognizable "root" parts that can help them unlock the meaning of an unfamiliar word. This activity gives students practice in applying an easy strategy to identify word parts and analyze them.

Materials:

A list of about 10 familiar compound words or a list of words that carry the same prefix or root. (The roots presented in Appendix A work well with this activity.) A "Divide and Conquer" sheet that has been prepared in advance and duplicated for each student. (See Appendix A for a template.)

Procedures:

1. Review the concept of "compound words" or prefixes by asking students to explain what is meant by a compound word (a single word that contains two or more complete words) or prefix (a unit added to the front of a word that affects its meaning; student responses will be simpler).

2. Write the word *birthday* on the board. Ask someone to explain what the word means. Now ask another student to identify what two words are in *birthday*. Ask how each of those words contributes to the meaning of the word *birthday* (a "birthday" is the day of your birth).

3. Show students the list of words and read the list together orally. Now ask students to choose a word on the list, tell what two words it contains and what it means. As students offer explanations, reinforce that the meaning of each compound word is built from the semantic relationship between the two units. (Here's a tip: The second word in a compound word usually describes the main idea. The first word gives a detail about the main idea.)

4. When all words on the list have been discussed, tell students that they have just used a strategy called "Divide and Conquer." Explain that words are made up of word parts or meaning units called *roots*. Tell students that when they meet an unknown word, they can figure out what it means by "dividing and conquering" its parts or "roots."

5. Now write these three compound words that use the word *book*: *bookcase, bookshelf, bookmark*. Ask students to divide and conquer each of these words. (A bookcase is a "case for books"; a bookshelf is a "shelf for books"; a bookmark "marks the book" where the reader left off.) As students offer explanations, note how the word *book* always has the same meaning. Remind students that the new word can be figured out by connecting the meaning of each word root.

6. Now distribute the "Divide and Conquer" template with the list of words with the same prefix or other compound words. Students will have a list of 10 words that can be used for a variety of extension activities that use art, drama, or writing.

CLUE Context Clues (Circle-Look-Underline-Explain)

Whenever students encounter unknown words, they can use this easy four-step strategy to predict the meaning of a new word based on the meaning of the surrounding passage.

Purpose:

To give students practice in using context clues to determine the meaning of unknown words. The activity deepens their awareness that the semantic and structural context in which a word appears offers clues about its meaning. It may be used as a whole-group, partner, or individual activity.

Materials:

A reading passage with four vocabulary words that will be new to most students or a sheet with four unrelated sentences (see Appendix A). Each sentence should include one word that will be new for most students.

Procedures:

1. Ask students to explain when, how, and why they use the strategy of context clues when reading. Emphasize that using context clues is a good method for figuring out the meaning of a word they do not know. Tell them you are going to show them an easy strategy called "CLUE" for using context clues to figure out the meaning of new words. Write "Circle, Look, Underline, Explain" on the board.

2. Now model the strategy. Write the sentence, "My dog enjoyed running at the canine park yesterday." CIRCLE the word *canine*. Ask students to help you LOOK at the rest of the sentence and figure out what words might provide a "clue" about the meaning of the word *canine*. UNDERLINE the words *dog, running,* and *park*. Then EXPLAIN how you think those words provide clues.

(For example, you might say "I know that dogs like to run outside. Parks are outdoor places for exercise. So a *canine* park must be a place especially for dogs to exercise. I bet that *canine* is another word for 'dog.'") Reinforce connections between the context clue words and your own prior knowledge. Reread the sentence and ask students if the meaning of "dog" makes sense.

3. Review the four steps you modeled. Now ask students to repeat this process with each of the sentences or the reading passage. Tell them to CIRCLE a word they don't know in each sentence. Next, ask them to LOOK at the rest of the sentence and UNDERLINE any words that are clues to the meaning of the unknown word. Then they must EXPLAIN what the word means and how the context helped.

4. Ask students to share their words and explanations with a partner or in whole-group discussion. Again, reinforce connections between the context clue words and students' prior knowledge. Remind students to use the CLUE strategy on their own when trying to figure out an unknown word in reading.

Cloze

This strategy (Rasinski & Padak, 2004) is frequently used to support reading comprehension, but it also is an excellent way to model and practice using context clues to determine word meanings. It is especially effective with Big Books or chart paper stories in a whole- or small-group setting.

Purpose:

To help develop readers' understanding and use of context clues by inviting students to predict words that have been omitted (or covered up) in a passage.

Materials:

A reading selection, either fiction or nonfiction, in which selected words have been omitted. This can be done as an independent activity, but a cloze sheet will need to be prepared and duplicated in advance.

Procedures:

1. Select a text that will challenge, but not overwhelm, your students. Identify several words that may easily be predicted from

the semantic context of the story. Leave the first and last sentences intact, so students have a mental framework. Cover the selected words with sticky notes, or omit the words if constructing a passage for duplication. (In a pure cloze, every fifth word is deleted, but how many and what words are omitted should depend entirely on your judgment of text difficulty and student need.)

2. Next, read the story to the students. Whenever you come to an omitted word, complete the reading of the sentence before you stop. If students are reading independently, tell them to read to the end of each sentence before looking for context clues.

3. Ask students to predict the meaning of each covered or omitted word. As each word is discussed, make sure that the students describe the strategies they used to figure out the correct word. Asking students to talk about their own strategy use deepens metacognitive awareness. Point out the variety of different clues students used as well as the importance of connecting their prior knowledge.

Word Mapping

With this strategy, students analyze a word by "mapping" it with a definition and a sketch before using it in a sentence. Defining and sketching lay a conceptual framework about the word. Using it in the context of a sentence they have generated deepens their understanding, particularly if they share maps with each other. This works well with the whole group when introducing a word. It is equally effective when children select their own words to map and then share those with others.

Purpose:

To deepen students' conceptual and contextual knowledge as they explore one word from different visual and contextual perspectives.

Materials:

A list of words for a topic under study. A reading selection, either fiction or nonfiction. Use the Word Mapping template (see Appendix A).

Procedures:

1. Begin by modeling how to construct a word map using an overhead transparency of the Word Mapping template. Select a word

that you think most students will already know. Write the word in the center of the map. Tell students they will fill in the map by following the numbers and answering the questions in each box. Ask students to help you write a definition in the first box, which says "1. This word means . . . ."

2. Now ask them to go to box 2 which says, "It looks like . . . ." Briefly talk about what you might draw and then make a quick sketch in the box. Continue this process with boxes 3 and 4, which ask you to write and illustrate a sentence that includes the word.

3. After you have modeled the process, invite students to select a word (or provide words) and do a map on their own.

4. Encourage students to share their completed maps. When students have worked on the same word, point out the different contexts in which it can be used. When students have worked on different words, encourage questions about why they chose their word. Talking about the words is a good way to give students practice using them.

Word Pyramids

This popular strategy, adapted from Nickelsen (1998), invites students to build a pyramid from synonyms and antonyms. Students first analyze a word by identifying individual words that have similar and opposite meanings, but the foundation of their pyramid is a sentence in which they use the word in a meaningful context. This activity can be done as a whole group or individually. It also works well as a partner activity. Either way, it is important to have students share pyramids.

Purpose:

To deepen students' conceptual and contextual knowledge as they explore one word from different perspectives.

Materials:

A list of words for a topic under study. A reading selection, either fiction or nonfiction. Use the Word Pyramid template (see Appendix A).

Procedures:

1. Begin by reviewing the concepts of "synonym" (words with similar meaning) and "antonym" (words with opposite meaning).

2. Then model how to construct a word pyramid on an overhead transparency. Choose a word that you think most students will

already know. Write the word in the first blank at the top. Tell students they will complete the pyramid by filling in the blanks.

3. The second line asks for two antonyms. Ask students to help you brainstorm antonyms. Choose two to fill in the banks.

4. Now repeat the process, looking for synonyms to fill in the third line. Ask for suggestions and then choose three.

5. Continue this process with the fourth line, which asks for a definition. Again, invite discussion and decide on a four-word definition.

6. Finally, students are asked to write a sentence that is two lines long. After you have modeled the process, invite students to select a word (or provide words) and do a pyramid on their own.

7. Encourage students to share their word pyramids. When students have worked on the same word, point out the variety of ways in which it can be used. When students have worked on different words, encourage questions about why they chose their word. Talking about the words is a good way to give students practice using them.

Word Spokes

This strategy (Rasinski, Padak, Newton, & Newton, 2007) is a twist on Word Pyramids, but it is specifically designed to help students build words from word roots and prefixes. It works well as a follow-up to "Divide and Conquer" and can be done individually, as a group, or as a partner activity.

Purpose:

To develop students' word analysis skills by manipulating word roots.

Materials:

An age-appropriate list of familiar prefixes or word roots (Appendix A). Use the Word Spokes template (see Appendix A).

Procedures:

1. Begin by reviewing the concept that sometimes words are made up of recognizable "root" parts that give us clues about what a word means. Write the prefix *re-*, or choose another familiar prefix. Tell students that *re* always means "back," and that they can figure out the meaning of lots of *re-* words by keeping that in mind. Tell them that they are going to build many *re-* words in an activity called "Word Spokes."

34
....

CHAPTER 2

*Instructional
Strategies for
Vocabulary
Development*

2. Put a blank Word Spokes template on an overhead transparency. Before filling in the spokes, you might want to ask students what image they get when they think of "spokes" (e.g., a wheel with spokes). Write the prefix *re-* in the center circle, and tell students that they must "spoke" out five different words that have the prefix *re-*.

3. As students call out words, write a different *re-* word in each spoke.

4. Direct students' attention to the questions, and tell them that now they need to answer some questions about each of the words they have put in each spoke.

5. Guide them through the questions. Students are asked to find synonyms, find antonyms, write a definition, and write a sentence, but they must use a different word from the spokes for each question.

6. Students can answer the last question by choosing which of the four ways they want to present the remaining word. Papers can also be traded with a neighbor, who then answers the last question.

7. When you have finished modeling the strategy, students can do their own Word Spokes with roots they choose or you assign. When students have worked on the same root, point out the variety of words and the ways in which those words can be used. When students have worked on different roots, encourage questions about how they chose their words. Talking about the words is a good way to give students practice using them.

Inviting Word Exploration and Play

One of the most important ways you can "teach" vocabulary is to provide regular opportunities for your students to discover and practice words on their own or in the company of others. Research tells us that for students to master a word, they need to meet it multiple times in conversation or through reading and writing (Blachowicz & Fisher, 2002). Create a classroom setting that stimulates word curiosity and word exploration by making time for students to explore and play word games on their own or with others. Remember that words themselves are just plain interesting, and your ultimate goal is to create lifelong word-lovers. Giving students time to play "Wordo," the well-known "Hangman," and "Twenty Questions" is not only fun—it's good instruction.

The following strategies provide opportunities for students to investigate, discover, and share interesting words. Some of them challenge students by manipulating letter patterns. You will find that all these activities are highly motivational and will quickly become classroom favorites.

Word Jars

Jeff Barger (2006) was a third-grade teacher when he developed this strategy in which students collect and share interesting words.

Purpose:

To broaden students' experience with words and foster awareness that interesting words are to be found in many different places.

Materials:

A small plastic jar and strips of paper for each student. (Another option is to give each student a wire shower curtain ring and index cards.)

Procedures:

1. Tell students they are to become word detectives, searching out new words that are interesting to them. Ask students to talk about all the places where they might hear or find new words (at home, reading, watching television). Make a list of all the different places students might locate interesting words.

2. Then give each student a small plastic jar and a set of paper strips. Tell them they are to keep this jar handy as a place to collect their own words. Every night the students are asked to write one word they found interesting and discuss the meaning of it with their families.

3. Make sure parents know about this activity. You may want to put a note in the jar, explaining that their children will be looking for words that are unfamiliar and interesting to them. Ask parents to spend a few minutes each night listening to the word their child has chosen for the day.

4. Designate a time for students to bring the jars back to class to share and trade words with classmates. (This is a good Friday afternoon activity!)

Barger (2006) says that "in order to fill their slips of paper, children read soup labels, macaroni boxes, and other nontraditional sources of language. Words like *artificial* and *scrumptious* have become part of our vocabulary through visual reminders such as vocabulary-themed bulletin boards and word walls" (p. 280). Barger adds that this activity is "a good way to remind students that text exists everywhere, not just in books" (p. 280). After a few weeks, you will have lots of words that can be used for a variety of extension activities. Words can also be organized into many different kinds of categories (see List-Group-Label earlier in this chapter).

"Words for the Day" (Rasinski & Padak, 2004) is a variation of "Word Jars" in which children start each day by sharing words they found particularly interesting the day before. Their words can come from anywhere, but students must tell how they found them, why they chose them, and what they think each word means. The list remains up all day, and students are encouraged to use the words as much as possible that day.

The daily list can also be used for a variety of extension activities. Over time, lists can be posted or collected in one corner of the room. Students can then refer to words from previous days and weeks when they are looking for interesting words to use for other purposes, such as writing a story.

"Root of the Week" is another variation of "Word Jars" and "Words for the Day." This one focuses attention on words that share a prefix or root word. Ask students to be on the lookout for words they encounter that contain a specific root-of-the-week. Post a chart with the root in bold letters at the top. Number each line. Tell students that whenever they discover a word with that root, they should add it to the list. Tell them to (1) write the word, (2) circle the word part, and (3) write where the word was found. At the end of the week, review the list. Students love hunting for these words, so you may find your class filling more than one sheet each week. Find a spot in the room to collect all the charts. As the weeks pass, you will have many lists of words you can use for different purposes.

Wordo

This vocabulary version of Bingo (Rasinski, Padak, Newton, & Newton, 2007) is a wonderful way for students to play with new words they are learning.

Purpose:

Students experience an age-appropriate group of words through simultaneous use of oral and written language.

Materials:

A list of 12 to 16 words and a Wordo card for each child (see Appendix A).

Procedures:

1. Write the words you have chosen on the board.

2. Duplicate and pass out a Wordo card to each student. Ask each student to choose a free box and mark it. Then have them write one of the words in each of the remaining boxes. Students choose whatever box they wish for each word. (If you give them more than 11 words, some of the words will not be chosen.)

3. Now call a clue for each word. The clue can be the definition for the word, a synonym, an antonym, or a sentence with the target word deleted. Students need to figure out the correct target word, then put an X through it. (If you want to clear the sheets and play again, use small scraps of paper or other items to mark the squares.) When a student has four Xs in a row, column, diagonal, or four corners, he or she calls out "Wordo." (For very young children, or those playing for the first time, you may want to simplify the process by saying the word and then asking them to mark it.)

4. Check the words and declare that student the winner. Then have students clear their sheets and play another round of Wordo. The winner of the first game can be the one to call out clues.

Twenty Questions

The vocabulary version of this popular game uses oral language and personal connections to deepen conceptual knowledge.

Purpose:

Students take turns asking questions that will help them figure out a "mystery" word. If you want to build a little competitive spirit, you can divide the class into two teams for this activity.

Materials:

A list of words from a chart or word wall, or a paper bag with at least a dozen words on slips of paper. Words can be from a reading selection or topic the class is studying.

Procedures:

1. If students have never played "Twenty Questions," review the rules for them. Indicate the list of words. Tell students that one of them will get to be "it." That student will choose a word that classmates will try to guess by asking questions. If no one can figure out the word after 20 questions have been asked, then the student who is "it" will reveal the word.

2. If someone guesses the correct word, that person becomes "it" and gets to choose the next word. Remind students that the person who is "it" can answer only "yes" or "no" to their questions. You may want to scaffold this by taking the first turn as "it" yourself. Otherwise, invite someone to begin. Then let students take over, asking questions until someone has guessed the correct word.

3. Repeat the process. This game can take as much or as little time as you choose. It's a quick filler or Friday afternoon wind-down activity.

Root Word Riddles

Who doesn't enjoy the brain-teasing process of solving a riddle? This strategy (Rasinski, Padak, Newton, & Newton, 2007) invites students to create and guess riddles with words from the same root. Students get to think "outside the box" as they try to guess a word by connecting semantic clues.

Purpose:

To broaden students' knowledge of vocabulary words from the same root. This works well as a partner or team activity.

Materials:

A list of 6 to 10 words from the targeted root or word part. Chart paper. Students will need paper and a pencil.

Procedures:

1. Begin by reviewing the meaning of the root. Read the list of words together. Next, ask students to explain what each word means. Make sure their explanation includes the meaning of the root.

2. If students have not created riddles before, share some riddles with them. There are many good books of riddles from which

to choose. Spend some time not only solving riddles but also talking about how riddles are constructed. Ask students what kind of clues seem particularly helpful.

3. Now pick a word from the list and tell students you will create a riddle for them to guess. Tell them you are going to give them three clues. Write out the first clue. Make sure to begin it with the words "*I mean . . . .*" Then write out a second and third clue. (Example of clues for the word *invisible:* I mean something you cannot see. My opposite is "visible." I have four syllables. What am I?)

4. Then ask students to select a word from the list and make their own riddle to share with others.

5. Finally, spend some time swapping riddles. When students have written riddles about the same word, point out the variety of clues and the ways in which the word can be described. Note how each of the words shares a certain meaning based on its common root.

Scattergories

Rasinski and Padak's (2004) version of the popular board game is a wonderful way to use the skill of categorization to build vocabulary.

Purpose:

To broaden students' conceptual knowledge by connecting vocabulary words to specific categories. This works especially well as a partner or team activity.

Materials:

A list of five categories that will generate many words (e.g., vegetables, countries, animals). The categories can be developed from themes or content areas. Duplicate the Scattergories template for each child (see Appendix A).

Procedures:

1. Begin by telling students you will give them five categories and a set of letters. They will have a few minutes to brainstorm as many words as they can for each category, but all the words will have to begin with one of the letters. You may want to use an overhead transparency of the Scatttergories matrix to help students visualize the process.

40
....

CHAPTER 2

*Instructional
Strategies for
Vocabulary
Development*

2. Tell students to copy one category in each box at the top. Now tell them to write the letters you have selected, putting one in each box down the side.

3. Now tell them they have five minutes, working individually or in teams, to think of as many words as they can that begin with the given letters and fit the category. Remind students to write all the words they think of that begin with the same letter in one box.

4. When time is up, ask students to share words. The player or team with the greatest number of words wins.

"Alphaboxes" (Hoyt, 1999) is a variation of Scattergories that can be done in teams or as a whole group. In this version, students brainstorm a word for every letter of the alphabet. The words are related to a topic or a book that has been read. (If the topic is "animals," for example, students might brainstorm "ant, bear, cat, dog, elephant," etc.) Students can generate as many topic-related words as they can think of for each letter. Use the template in Appendix A for students to use or make an alphabox chart that the class fills in together. A class chart will generate many words that can be used for a variety of extension activities.

Further Word Exploration

You can quickly develop additional strategies for word exploration by adapting some of the familiar activities students already enjoy. Here are a few ideas to get you started:

- After reading a story, ask students to revisit it and then *sketch* a few words they found interesting. Tell them to share these with others who try to guess what words they have drawn.

- Provide sets of four words, but make sure that only three are related. Ask students to decide which one doesn't belong with the others. Then ask students to explain why that one is the *"odd word out."*

- Create a board game like "Memory" for students to play with each other—just substitute interesting words for pictures!

- Adapt card games like "Go Fish" for word study. Just make a deck of word cards with sets of four related words (e.g., *look, looks, looking, looked; return, rewind, rethink, refund*).

- Challenge students with crossword puzzles, word searches, jumbles, and word ladders. See Chapter 5 for Internet sites that will help you make your own. You can also purchase commercial versions of these activities that can be duplicated for students. Several of our favorites are also listed in Chapter 5.
- Make sure word exploration resources (e.g., dictionaries) and word games your students can play are easily accessible on your classroom computers. See Chapter 5 for a list of Internet sites your students will enjoy using.

As you can see, the study of word meanings must be an ongoing and natural part of daily classroom life. Your vocabulary instructional routines should include strategies that help students (1) build conceptual knowledge, (2) analyze word parts, and (3) deepen their word awareness through independent and collaborative word exploration.

Since many of the new words students will meet come from the texts they read, it may be useful to think about this three-pronged approach as it unfolds before, during, and after reading instruction:

Before Reading: Build Concepts

- Teach students how to *connect prior knowledge* with unfamiliar concepts. Use what they already know about life and language to introduce new vocabulary.

During Reading: Word Analysis

- Teach students how to unlock meaning through the use of *context clues* and *word "root" parts.*

After Reading: Word Talk

- Include conversation about interesting words students found in the text as a regular part of group discussion.
- Enhance metacognitive awareness by asking students to share how they figured out any difficult words.

Some combination of whole-class instruction and focused individualized work is probably the best way to organize the vocabulary portion of your reading program. Consider the diverse needs of your students when making specific plans. Evidence-based strategies and instructional guidelines, such as those discussed in this chapter, can provide you with direction for effective vocabulary instruction.

Materials for vocabulary instruction and practice are abundant. Look through children's literature and you will find stories full of rich, "juicy" words. You will find many wonderful books and series that feature word play. Many of these texts, such as the *Amelia Bedelia* series, will teach your students new words while also teaching them about the nature of words at the same time. If you use a basal reading program, supplement words in the teacher's guide by inviting students to look for words they find interesting as they read.

Commercial programs that build vocabulary are also available. In evaluating these, we recommend that you focus on the following questions:

- Is there a logic to the vocabulary being studied? Are the words appropriate for your students' developmental level? Check out the rationale for how words were selected. Is the rationale consistent with what you know about how children learn language?
- Will your students find the activities engaging? Are the activities developmentally appropriate?
- Do the activities provide regular opportunity for your students to build and deepen their conceptual knowledge?
- Do your students get to learn and apply word analysis strategies, particularly the study of word roots and context clues?
- Do the children have regular opportunities to use oral language (e.g., discussion) focused around vocabulary study?
- Are there opportunities for metacognitive growth?
- Do the children have a chance to explore words independently and in the company of others?
- Do your students have frequent opportunities to stretch their understanding of words through playful activities such as crossword puzzles and word ladders?
- Is the program intended for the range of readers that you teach?
- Does the program offer strategies to differentiate instruction so that all learners can grow?
- Are a variety of scaffolding practices available for the children who need it?
- Is the amount of time per day appropriate (10 to 15 minutes daily)?
- Is the overall instructional routine appropriate?
- Does the program fit well with the rest of your literacy curriculum?
- Are assessment ideas offered?

Professional Development Suggestions

Book Club

Discussion Questions

Work with two other teachers, ideally at your own grade level. First, select two issues from the list that follows. Then, each of you should make individual notes about the issue. Third, share these notes with each other. Spend some time talking through the issue. See if you can reach consensus about how to resolve it. Make notes about this discussion. Finally, share insights with others in your whole group.

- How can we evaluate the usefulness of our current materials for vocabulary instruction?

  _____

  _____

  _____

  _____

- How much vocabulary instruction should be whole-group oriented? How much small-group instruction? What kinds of groups? How much individual work? And, for all of the above, why?

  _____

  _____

  _____

  _____

- What key math, social studies, and science concepts are children expected to learn in your classroom? For each content area, make a list of the key vocabulary for these concepts and then list ways that you can help children learn these concepts.

  _____

  _____

  _____

  _____

- How can you explain your vocabulary program to parents?

  _____

  _____

  _____

  _____

CHAPTER 3

Assessing Vocabulary Development

Big Ideas

In each of the books in this series, we have identified several "big ideas" to guide your thinking about assessment. These big ideas apply to assessing all aspects of literacy learning (indeed, to all learning), but the comments and examples below frame them in the context of assessing children's vocabulary growth.

- *Focus on critical information.* Aim for a direct connection between what you need to know and the assessment tools/strategies you use. You can decide about critical information by considering the broad definition of vocabulary that was presented earlier in this book. Keep in mind that vocabulary knowledge is more than mastery of the definitional meaning of a particular set of words. Knowing a word involves both conceptual and contextual knowledge.

Furthermore, "contextual" knowledge has many layers. Teachers tend to think of "context" primarily as a strategy for using the structural and semantic background of a passage to figure out an unknown word. But "context" also includes the different environments in which we use words. When you are at home, for example, you typically choose words that communicate practical information or express your feelings to family members who share the same backgrounds and experiences. But the vocabulary of school is quite specialized, requiring even young students to understand and generate words they do not often hear outside of school. Many of the words used in school represent abstract concepts that are new to many students. Moreover, even words students do hear at home are sometimes used differently in school. Consider Mrs. Wishy-Washy's (Cowley, 1990) delightful expression, "Oh lovely mud!" How many of your students will have heard the word *lovely* used to describe "mud"? So, in addition to thinking about the different kinds of vocabulary your students know, you will need to consider the depth and breadth of their word knowledge. How fluid is their understanding of a word? Can they adapt what they know about a word to determine what it means when they encounter it in new print and oral contexts?

Keeping all these concerns in mind, now think about your own students. Identify a student whose vocabulary is particularly impressive. Try making a list of his or her observable indicators—why does she or he stand out?

Is it the number and kind of words the student uses?

Does the student use a variety of interesting and descriptive words when speaking or writing stories?

Does the child's vocabulary indicate a solid bank of conceptual knowledge on a variety of topics?

Are there specific words that are challenging for others that this particular student uses correctly? If so, why might that be?

Is the student particularly skilled at using context clues and word roots?

Does the child take pleasure in words, enjoy word games, and listen to stories with playful language like puns and riddles?

Is the child curious about words, asking questions and independently pursuing answers from many sources?

Once you have thought about the many dimensions of word knowledge and your own students, you can decide on the critical information you will need to get. McTighe and Wiggins (2004) suggest that this process works best when it begins at the end: (1) if the desired result is for learners to _____, (2) then assessment should provide you with evidence of _____, (3) and so assessment tasks need to include something like _____.

• *Look for patterns of behavior.* Rob Tierney (1998) notes that assessment "should be viewed as ongoing and suggestive, rather than fixed or definitive" (p. 385). No one instance can possibly tell you what you need to know about a child's vocabulary. Situations make a difference, as do practice, difficulty level of the material, and a host of other factors. So, your goal should be to determine children's vocabulary development by looking for patterns of growth over time. To do this, you need a plan. Get baseline information about children at the beginning of the year. Then select a few children on which to focus each week. Don't limit yourself to watching how well they use new vocabulary. Make your approach comprehensive: Observe all their "word ways," noticing word choice and flexibility when they talk, read, and write. Make notes about what you observe. Some of this will be routine, but you may also want to select children about whom you need more information or children whose current behavior is surprising in some way (Rasinski & Padak, 2004).

• *Recognize developmental progressions (can't, can sometimes, can always) and attend to children's cultural or linguistic differences.* Tierney (1998) advises that "assessment should be more developmental and sustained than piecemeal and shortsighted" (p. 384). "I envision . . . assessments that build upon, recognize, and value rather than displace what students have experienced in their worlds" (p. 381). Your plans should be sensitive to both of these issues. With regard to the former, for example, children may first recognize a word before they are able to use it easily. When they hear the word *lovely* in the context of Mrs. Wishy-Washy, most children will easily grasp its essential meaning. Without considerable exposure and practice, however, they will probably not use it themselves. With regard to the latter, cultural differences will influence what words some children hear and use. Many children for whom English is a second language will never have heard some of the idiomatic expressions others take for granted, so it will be important to know about both the linguistic and nonverbal cultures your students have been immersed in at home and in their communities.

• *Be parsimonious.* The question: How much assessment information do you need? The answer: Enough to help you make good instructional decisions. One way to conceptualize this quantity-of-information question is to think in terms of three related layers of assessment information.

At the top of the figure is what is done for and with all students in the class. Begin with a broad plan to assess children's vocabulary at the beginning of the year and then, perhaps, quarterly. Then think

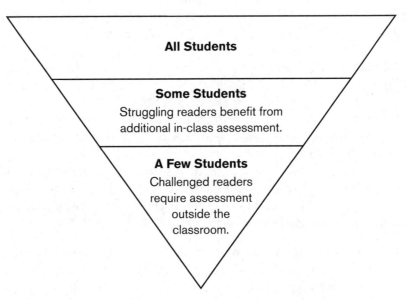

Source: Rasinski and Padak (2004, p. 277). Reprinted by permission of Pearson Education, Inc.

about results—what (or whom) do you still have questions about? This is the point to move to the second layer of the triangle. Here, you will do more focused (and time-consuming) vocabulary assessments. You might work individually with a child, perhaps more of what you've already done or a "deeper" assessment. For example, you might assess a child's vocabulary with easier material on a topic you have studied in class. Or you might make use of assisted situations (where you read a passage to the child and then ask him or her a simple question about a particular word: "How can mud be called 'lovely'?"). If you still have questions, don't hesitate to ask for outside help. A child or two in the class may benefit from a diagnosis by a reading specialist or other highly specialized professional. Don't delay and don't hesitate. Every lost day represents lost opportunities for that child's learning. Above all, keep assessments at these different layers related to one another, focused on the same key vocabulary issues.

- *Use instructional situations for assessment purposes.* Tierney (1998) notes that ideally, "assessments should emerge from the classroom rather than be imposed upon it" (p. 375). We can think of two good reasons for this stance, one conceptual and the other practical. From a conceptual perspective, you want to know how children behave in typical instructional situations. After all, a major purpose of assessment is to provide instructional guidance. From a practical standpoint, gathering assessment information from instruction saves time for your teaching and children's learning. Children don't learn much of value during testing sessions. To evaluate your vocabulary instruction for possible assessment situations, you might begin by listing the instructional opportunities that children have to explore words. Then develop a plan to capture observations about children's vocabulary during instruction. Above all, take Karen West's (1998) advice to heart: "I want instruction and evaluation to be in meaningful authentic contexts" (p. 550).

- *Include plans for (1) using assessment information to guide instruction and (2) sharing assessment information with children and their parents.* The last step of your assessment planning might be to double-check ideas against their primary purposes: to help you teach more effectively and to communicate your insights with children and their parents. With regard to the former, it may be particularly important to think about how you can adjust instruction for children who appear to be struggling with word analysis strategies. Can you provide easier texts for them or build extra vocabulary support into their instructional days? In addition, consider how you can share information about vocabulary with children and their parents. Knowing that they are making progress will keep children engaged in their learning. Assessment conversations are also good ways to help children develop more abstract concepts about the semantic aspect of word study. And parents, of course, are both interested in their children's progress in school and frequently willing to assist in their children's education. Rob Tierney (1998) reminds us that it is important to keep parents informed, but more than that, involved: "Rather than keep the parent or caregiver at arm's length . . . , we need to embrace the concerns that parents have and the contributions they can make" (p. 380).

Evaluate Your Current Assessment Practices

The two accompanying charts may help you take a careful look at your current assessment practices in vocabulary. The first chart considers the broad instructional areas we have identified as central to vocabulary instruction. The second chart identifies specific student behaviors that support vocabulary growth. To complete the charts, first list all the ways you currently assess students' vocabularies in the "Assessment Tool/Strategy" column. Then consider the information each tool or strategy provides about each of the critical aspects by marking the chart: + = excellent source of information; – = some information; blank = no information. When the charts are complete, make plans for revision. Are some critical aspects receiving too much/not enough attention? Can some tools/strategies be eliminated or revised? What revisions will enhance your overall assessment strategies?

Critical Aspects: Vocabulary Instruction

Assessment Tool/Strategy	Key Words: Concepts	Word Analysis: Roots	Word Analysis: Context	Oral Language: Discussion	Written Language: Composition	Word Awareness: Exploration

Critical Indicators: Vocabulary Development

Assessment Tool/Strategy	Decodes Words Already in Meaning Vocabulary	Learns New Concepts (or labels for concepts)	Uses New Vocabulary Orally and in Writing	Applies Strategies to Learn New Words (structure, semantics, metacognition)	Uses Reference Works and Other Resources to Learn New Words

Notes about revisions:

What did you conclude by analyzing your current strategies for assessing vocabulary? Perhaps you are satisfied that you have enough of the right kind of information about your students. If not, you may find some of the following ideas helpful for supplementing your plans.

Observation Charts

You can duplicate charts like the ones on the next page to use at times when children are showing their proficiency with oral and written language. You can make brief notes on the chart or use some kind of symbol system, such as O = Outstanding, S = Satisfactory, and U = Unsatisfactory. Since assessing children in this way once every month or two may provide enough information, you can focus on different students each week and, over time, observe all your students.

Observation Chart

Indicator	Child's Name	Child's Name	Child's Name	Child's Name
Decodes words already in meaning vocabulary				
Learns new concepts (or labels for concepts)				
Uses new vocabulary orally and in writing				
Applies strategies to learn new words (structure, semantics, metacognition)				
Uses reference works and other resources to learn new words				

Observation Chart

Aspect	Child's Name	Child's Name	Child's Name	Child's Name
Concepts				
Word roots				
Context clues				
Discussion				
Composition				
Word exploration				

Use Instructional Activities

Some instructional activities have vocabulary assessment value. Several that work particularly well are described next. (See Rasinski & Padak, 2004, for more detailed descriptions of the first four activities.) Although no single occasion will provide a complete picture of a child's vocabulary knowledge and ability, notes about performance with these may be useful. You might want to create a chart with children's names down one side and activities/dates across the other; you can then use the O-S-U notation system to summarize children's performance.

- *List-Group-Label.* Select a topic for study. Tell students to brainstorm all the words they can that are related to the topic. List these words for the children, who then work in small groups to categorize the words and label the resulting categories. Whole-group sharing concludes the lesson. If this activity is used before reading or studying a topic, assessing children's products provides a good indication of prior conceptual knowledge. If it is used as a culminating activity, products show concept learning.

- *Word Sorts.* Select about 20 words or phrases from a text students will read. Write the words on individual cards or slips of paper, then give sets of words to pairs of students. Students group the words into categories that make sense to them (open word sort) or categories that you provide (closed word sort). As with List-Group-Label, students' word sorts can provide information about their vocabulary knowledge, either before or after they read.

- *Important Words.* As (or after) they read, students identify words in a selection they consider to be important. These are shared in small groups, after which students might (1) create maps or webs of the group's words, (2) categorize them, or (3) discuss the words and come to group consensus about which are the most important (and why). Students' facility with concepts can be assessed through observation during this activity. Products will also provide assessment information.

- *Wide Reading.* This activity is an excellent way to increase vocabulary (Blachowicz & Fisher, 2004; Nagy & Herman, 1987; National Reading Panel, 2000). Indeed, the NRP notes the importance of the "indirect" word learning that results from wide reading (or listening—teacher read-aloud has a role here as well). You can ask students to keep dated lists of books they have read. You can assess these lists occasionally to determine how much "wide reading" students are doing. Perhaps students can also jot down a few new or interesting or important words from each of the books they read. These lists, too, can provide informal assessment information.

• *Expressing Thought.* Using vocabulary to express a thought requires a deeper understanding than figuring out a potential meaning when a word is encountered in print. "Sentence Starters" (adapted from Nickelsen, 1998) and "Words Knew and New" (adapted from Rasinski, Padak, Newton, & Newton, 2007) give students practice using vocabulary in new contexts, while giving you a snapshot of their conceptual understanding. For "Sentence Starters," provide a list of vocabulary words and a "generic" phrase to begin a sentence. Students complete each sentence by choosing one (or more) of the words from the list.

Sentence Starters

....

Words: dark   follow   answer   important   mountain   complete
waves   scientist

1. While I was trying to **_complete_** *my story I got stuck.*
2. How do you know if *you have the right* **answer?**
3. Where in the world can *a* **scientist** *find a dinosaur today?*
4. What would you think about *climbing a very big* **mountain?**
5. Why should *you be careful walking in the* **dark?**

Variations of this include changing the initial prompts and limiting or expanding the number of word choices you provide. You may also want to ask students to use more than one word in each sentence.

Similarly, "Words Knew and New" invites students to choose words and apply them in new contexts. Students choose, define, and use familiar and unfamiliar words from a reading selection or a list you provide. Students must also explain why they chose those particular words. This activity provides the children with vocabulary practice and fosters metacognitive awareness; it gives you a snapshot of their conceptual knowledge and word analysis strategies. You can duplicate the template in Appendix A. The template may also be used to guide an oral conference. You then provide a list of words the children can choose from as they respond to your questions.

Words Knew and New

1. Choose a word whose meaning you already know. Write the word. What does it mean?

   Parachute.   It is something used in jumping from a plane.

2. Choose a word you find very interesting that you did not know before. Write the word. What does it mean? Why do you find it interesting?

   *Toot.   It means a sound like a horn. It's interesting because it sounds
   funny.*

3. Select a new word you think is very hard. Write the word. What do you think it means? Tell why you think it is hard. How did you figure it out?

   *Biplane.   It is a plane that has two wings. I never saw one before, so it
   was interesting. The picture helped me figure it out.*

4. Write one sentence with two of the three words you chose.

   If a biplane crashes, a parachute could save your life.

5. Now write one sentence with the remaining word.

   We had to toot our horn at the dog in the road.

- *Odd Word Out.* One way to make the meaning of a word clear is to compare how it is similar to or different from other words. This quick teacher-constructed assessment from Rasinski, Padak, Newton, and Newton (2007) asks students to choose which word does not "fit" and then explain why. Through classification and analysis, students build their conceptual knowledge while you assess their understanding. This activity can be used as a paper-and-pencil activity or as a discussion prompt during an informal conference. If used in an oral conversation, keep anecdotal records or a checklist that can track students' growth in classification skills over time.

Odd Word Out

Look at the four words. Write the one that doesn't belong on the line. Then write how the other words are the same.

> precook
> preheat
> premixed
> pretest

The word that doesn't belong is _____. The other words are the same because _____.

> prehistoric
> preshrink
> presoak
> prewash

The word that doesn't belong is _____. The other words are the same because _____.

> premature
> premed
> premixed
> prenatal

The word that doesn't belong is _____. The other words are the same because _____.

To develop "Odd Word Out," select three or four words, two or three of which share some characteristic. Words could be related semantically or syntactically, or related by the presence or absence of word parts. Consider this example:

cat

dog

ant

tiger

The odd word could be *ant* because it is not a mammal, because it has more than four feet, or because it begins with a vowel. The odd word could also be *tiger* because it's not a three-letter word or because it has two syllables. The groups of words you select for "Odd Word Out" will often have multiple answers, which promotes children's thinking about the many ways in which words can be related to one another.

• *Matching.* One very simple and time-tested way of determining whether students understand a word is to ask them to select its synonym or antonym. Matching assessments can be developed very quickly. Number and list several words in a column down the left-hand side a page. Decide whether you want students to match a synonym or an antonym, then list those words in a column on the right-hand side. The children simply draw a line from the word to its correct match. Make sure to mix up the order so that the students will have to identify the correct match by reading through all the words in the column on the right. You can also have students match definitions, but this would take longer to construct. One variation is to add a few lines and ask students to choose three words and write a sentence for each. You can challenge older students by asking them to use more than one word in each sentence.

Matching

Draw a line from each word to its opposite.

deeper	easier
faster	later
harder	uglier
higher	shallower
sooner	slower
prettier	lower

Source: Rasinski, Padak, Newton, and Newton (2007).

• *Multiple-Choice Cloze.* The cloze strategy (Chapter 2) is one of the best ways to assess your students' use of context clues. A multiple-choice cloze (also called a "maze cloze") tests vocabulary knowledge by offering students a choice of words (Blachowicz & Fisher, 2006). In order to determine which is the correct word choice, students must draw on both definitional ("What does this word mean?") and contextual knowledge ("Does that meaning make sense in this passage?").

Multiple-Choice Cloze
....

She loved all pets, but thought that cats were especially nice because they were soft and easy to _____.

   cuddle   cure   confuse

Other Informal Assessment Ideas

Blachowicz and Fisher (2006) describe several informal vocabulary assessment techniques that are adaptable to many classroom contexts. Here are two especially good choices:

- *Knowledge Rating Charts.* Select key words from something your students will read. Make a three-column chart for students to indicate if they (1) know a word well, (2) have seen or heard it, or (3) don't know it at all. Blachowicz and Fisher note that this activity helps students come to understand "that knowing the meaning of a word is not something that happens all at once" (p. 100). Of course, observing students' responses can provide you with good assessment information as well.
- *One-Minute Meetings.* Select two or three key concepts from a unit of study. In brief individual conversations with students, discussions about these concepts provide information about the depth of students' knowledge.

Self-Assessment

Students can and should have some say in evaluating their own vocabulary growth. In addition to fostering students' sense of responsibility for their own learning, self-assessment is often motivating. Moreover, self-assessment sends a subtle reminder about the importance of words and word learning. Each time they assess themselves, students will think about vocabulary as an abstract concept. Over time, then, "word awareness" will become part of what they think about when they read. Ideas for self-assessment include:

- *Occasional Conversations.* You might begin by asking students to assess their understanding of a new vocabulary word after a read-aloud session: "What does _____ mean? What in the story helped you figure it out? How could you find out whether your understanding is correct? Can you think of any other words that have the same meaning?"

- *Peer Feedback.* When children are talking about words in discussion groups, sharing word-play activities such as crossword puzzles, or researching topics together on the Internet, they will encounter new words. As they compare their understanding, students will naturally articulate some of the strategies they are using to predict a meaning.

- *Journal Entries.* On occasion, ask children to write about their own word knowledge. You might want them to write definitions of new concepts in their own words, for example, or to reflect more broadly on the new words they have learned or on the value of word learning. Ask them to describe where they find new and interesting words. Also ask them to identify what strategies they use most often to figure out the meaning of new words. Prompts could include some of the checklist items mentioned above. Invite occasional discussions in which students offer comments about any of these issues based on their journal entries.

- *Counting Sight Words.* If students keep word banks of known words, ask them to count these words every four to six weeks. They can share these tallies with you and also keep track of them. Parents may be interested in this information as well.

- *Interesting Words.* Ask students to keep lists of interesting words they encounter in their reading. The entry for each word could also include its definition and student comments. Ask students to review these lists occasionally to draw some conclusions about their word knowledge.

Plans for Change

In this chapter, you have evaluated your own assessment strategies for vocabulary and, as a result, perhaps generated some ideas for change. Use the accompanying chart to make notes about the changes you wish to make. As you do so, make sure that these changes reflect the "big ideas" outlined at the beginning of the chapter:

- Focus on critical information.
- Look for patterns of behavior.
- Recognize developmental progressions and attend to children's cultural differences.
- Be parsimonious. (Which of your strategies will work for all of your students? Which might be reserved for more careful attention to some students' vocabulary needs?)
- Use instructional situations for assessment purposes.
- Include plans for (1) using assessment information to guide instruction and (2) sharing assessment information with children and parents.

You may want to share your plans with others to get their feedback.

Book Club

Goal Planning: Vocabulary Assessment

Goal _____

Plans by_____ Date _____

Action Steps: What do I need to do?	Materials/Resources	Evaluation: How will I assess the usefulness of this change?

CHAPTER 4

Beyond Strategies

*I*n earlier chapters, we explored how children learn to become word learners and some of the best instructional strategies to support that process. In this chapter, we will consider issues that go "beyond strategies." In particular, we address English language learners (ELLs) and provide guidelines and suggestions for at-home vocabulary activities.

ELL Students and Vocabulary Development

Did you ever study a foreign language in school? If so, you may recall feeling both excited and confused as you explored a whole new way of talking and thinking. This is how many children from other cultures feel as they enter U.S. classrooms. Given the cultural and linguistic diversity of the nation's population, your classroom may have children from several countries. How do you plan instruction that reaches each individual learner?

It is important to keep in mind that children raised in bilingual homes have unique advantages as well as unique challenges. These children bring rich background experiences that can be tapped to enhance everyone's learning. They know how to move between two languages, integrating sounds and meanings into new words and grammatical structures. Their natural manipulation of two languages promotes higher-level thinking. Yet, ELL students sometimes feel lost in the unfamiliar linguistic and academic world in which they find themselves. Fitzgerald and Graves (2004) describe this feeling:

> Many English-language learners bring an array of emotions to our classrooms that often are not evident on the surface. The student who is afraid that his talk will sound funny to others may hide his self-consciousness. The student who does not fully understand what is said may hold a steady gaze and outwardly appear confident or even cocky. (p. 3)

Fortunately, everything you have learned so far about how to teach vocabulary applies to both first and second language learners: ELL students need to focus on meaning, learn how to use context clues, analyze word roots, and develop word awareness by exploring new words on their own and in the company of others. Like all young learners, ELL students need to draw, write, read, and then talk about what they have drawn, written, or read with others. Because they are simultaneously learning how to speak, read, write, and think in a new language, these students must have continual opportunities to practice and try out new words in varied learning contexts. In general, ELL students usually require more scaffolding from you, especially in prereading activities. Following are some key ideas to keep in mind as you plan instruction for second language learners.

• *Build conceptual connections through prior knowledge.* Teachers know that activating and applying prior knowledge is central to all learning: As students compare new information with what they already know, they deepen their understanding of a topic. Second language learners, however, often lack basic content or conceptual knowledge in the texts teachers ask them to read. They also may not understand the vocabulary or idioms of English.

Imagine for a moment that you are in a country where everyone speaks Greek fluently, but you are just learning it. Someone tells you that "the lid tumbled and found the jar." Would you know they were describing a close relationship between two people? In English, we might describe this as being like "two peas in a pod," but would an ELL student automatically know what we mean? Try this popular Greek expression: "The grapevine was twisted and the donkey ate it." If you did not grow up in a region where a twisted grapevine was of significant concern, you might lack the conceptual knowledge to understand this description of a perilous situation. Such figurative expressions make a language rich and interesting, but can be quite bewildering to second language learners who may not know the meanings of idioms or who may lack important contextual information.

• *Use discussion to relate unfamiliar topics or concepts to similar topics or concepts in ELL students' lives.* A child from Ghana may not have direct experience of tornadoes but probably does understand the concept of a "natural disaster." After a prereading discussion introducing the concept of "tornado," you might ask ELL students what natural disasters are feared "in your country." The ensuing conversation will provide language practice for them and also expand the content knowledge of the other students who participate.

• *Use students' native language wherever possible.* Many English words have cognates in other languages. Because they share Latin derivatives, Spanish-speaking students can easily relate many new English words to Spanish. In introducing the word *aqueduct*, for example, students may already have the concept of "water" from the Spanish word *agua*. Encourage students to draw and share such connections between their first and second languages. As they discuss these cognates, everyone's awareness that English words are constructed from semantic units with "roots" in other languages will deepen. It might even yield a "teachable moment" to reinforce the strategy of "Divide and Conquer."

• *Preteach critical vocabulary.* Once you are confident that students have understood basic concepts, preteach vocabulary that is central to understanding the text. This can be tricky. Fitzgerald and Graves (2004) posit that if the concepts are familiar, ELL students can learn up to six new words before reading a text. They can handle only two or three new words if the concepts are unfamiliar. And remember that students will need lots of practice using those new words in multiple contexts before they really "own" them.

• *Frequently reinforce word learning strategies.* Students need to have a range of strategies that use the definitional, structural, and contextual features of words to build vocabulary (NRP, 2000; Stahl & Fairbanks, 1986). Context clues and word analysis ("roots") are probably the two most important. Unfortunately, since their attention is heavily focused on basic language processing, ELL students often forget to apply these strategies during reading. You may need to review strategies often, by using think-alouds or setting a "during reading" task, such as noting where a few key words you have discussed before reading appear in the text.

• *Provide explicit models of good language use.* Introduce a wide range of genres with different textual structures. Choose high-interest stories and poems to read to your students. Share picture books with playful or memorable words. Find good, interesting literature that will expand students' textual, content, and conceptual knowledge. This is important for all learners, but it is particularly helpful to ELL students. Some cultures, for example, do not use the problem-solution story structure that is popular in many school texts. Second language learners from such cultures would not automatically draw on this familiar structural framework to support their understanding of the text's meaning.

Furthermore, text selection can include topics and concepts that will give ELL students valuable background knowledge for school success. Find texts that build on concepts in your curriculum. Ask yourself whether the content will prompt a good discussion for oral language practice with new and familiar vocabulary. You will also want to help students choose stories and poems to read to themselves. The possibilities are endless.

• *Read challenging texts aloud.* Students' oral vocabulary is usually more extensive than their reading vocabulary. Reading a few paragraphs aloud to students before they read silently may help them understand the content. A few brief comments or questions about what you have read may also help students focus attention on important information in the passage. For second language learners, frequent opportunities to hear English texts read orally will build vocabulary, deepen comprehension, and model fluency.

- *Build a library of books, especially books about words!* Don't forget to stock your library with books at all reading levels and encourage students to choose and use them! Wordless picture books, which students can "read" by inventing stories with their available vocabulary, are particularly good for those children just beginning to speak English. In addition to enhancing their language skills, students will also be exposed to the story structures used most frequently in school texts.

Books *about* words are fascinating. They help students understand that each word comes to us with a unique history and structure. Picture books such as *Miss Alaineous: A Vocabulary Disaster* playfully reveal the complex nature of English spelling. And Amelia Bedelia's verbal peccadilloes (now there's an interesting word that your Spanish-speaking students might figure out easily!) have delighted generations of students. There are also plenty of books on the market that use word play with homophones, synonyms, riddles, puns, and even crossword puzzles.

Finally, have a variety of print and electronic dictionaries available. Make sure that some of them use pictures. Whenever possible, your collection should include attractive bilingual dictionaries that correspond to the first languages of the students in your classroom. Use the resources in Chapter 5 to get started!

Vocabulary Activities at Home

Both practitioners and researchers have long recognized the importance of parental involvement in children's early reading achievement. Results from nearly every National Assessment of Educational Progress have indicated that students who "regularly participate in literacy-related activities with their families have higher levels of reading achievement than students whose parents are not actively involved in their reading" (Rasinski & Padak, 2004, p. 240).

Children whose families encourage at-home literacy activities have higher phonemic awareness and decoding skills (Burgess, 1999), higher reading achievement in the elementary grades (Cooter, Marrin, & Mills-House, 1999), and advanced oral language development

(Senechal, LeFevre, & Thomas, 1998). Family literacy professionals often point out that parents are their children's first and most important teachers. Instructing parents to simply "read to your child" may be a start, but it is not enough. Parents need specific suggestions and guidelines about what to do and how to respond to their child's literacy development. In this section we offer guidelines and some sample activities for home involvement programs and practices that foster children's vocabulary development.

Teachers know that home involvement can provide rich opportunities for children to develop as readers. Moreover, it's important for children to see reading and literacy activities as worthwhile and critical outside of school as well as within school walls. Yet, home involvement programs are sometimes frustrating for teachers, parents, and children alike. Our work with supporting home involvement programs has led us to several design characteristics. These must be present for home involvement programs for young readers to be successful (Rasinski & Padak, 2004):

- *Use proven and effective strategies.* Many parents have limited time to devote to working with their children, so at-home activities must be focused on ideas that have been proven to make a positive difference in children's reading achievement.

- *Use authentic reading texts.* Reading aloud to children allows parents to model fluent reading as well as point out text features. Similarly, when parents read with their children or listen to their children read, children grow as readers. These simple activities—read to, read with, and listen to children—are powerful ways to promote reading achievement. For optimal vocabulary development, emphasize an additional activity: *talk!* Tell parents to ask their children questions that begin with "I wonder," "I think," and "I like" to get the conversation going. After exchanging some thoughts about the content of the story, parents can point out an interesting word or two—and ask their children to do the same. What about texts? We believe it's essential for them to be authentic. For young readers, texts such as simple poems, song lyrics, jokes, or jump-rope rhymes work very well.

- *Provide materials.* Some parent involvement plans fail because parents lack appropriate texts or the time or resources to acquire them. The easiest solution is to provide parents and children with reading materials. In addition to looking for materials in books, teachers will find the Internet a treasure trove of wonderful materials for children and parents to read. (See resources listed in Chapter 5 for examples.)

With these principles in mind, you can develop some simple home vocabulary activities. Suggestions include the following:

- Talk to parents about the importance of embedding *word awareness* in their children's literacy experiences. Explain that word awareness is really curiosity about words, where they come from, what they mean, and how they can be used. Make sure parents understand that you are not referring to rote memorization of a specific list of "important" words. Instead, you want their children to establish a habit-of-mind about words. Suggest that parents occasionally comment about an unusual word or expression they have run across. Tell parents to wonder out loud about the meaning of a new word they hear and to encourage their children to do the same. They can engage in a brief discussion about the word and then take a moment to look it up together in a dictionary or on the Internet.

- Encourage parents to make trips to the local library a regular part of their routine. Emphasize that we learn most new vocabulary through reading, and we read more widely when we choose books of high interest to us. Urge parents to allow enough time for their children to browse through and choose from the hundreds of appealing children's books available on the shelves. You may want to tell them about other literacy resources available at the library, including computers, videos, and "reading" rooms. In most libraries, children and adults can also participate in book clubs. Some libraries even have family book clubs where parent and child read the same book. These are wonderful occasions for shared and joyful language experiences.

- Show parents how to do paired reading with their children. Make sure they pause now and then to talk about the story. When they have finished, remind parents to ask their child to describe a favorite part or favorite character. Then tell them to go back, find an interesting word, and invite their child to find one too.

- Draw up a list of easy, playful word games children and parents can do together. "Twenty Questions," "Hangman," and "Charades" are perennial favorites that will give everyone a mental "word stretch." Older children will enjoy inventing riddles to stump family members. Where can students find good words to use in these games? Everywhere, really. If you want to give parents more structure, though, revisit "Word Jars" in Chapter 2 for instructions on how to make your students "word detectives" as they collect and store interesting words they hear at home. In a few short weeks, children will have plenty of words from which to choose.

- Don't forget about the many resources available for word games on the Internet. In Chapter 5 you will find several websites that students can access on home computers. There are excellent electronic versions of many popular games, including "Hangman," "Memory," and "Concentration," that will keep children fascinated with vocabulary for hours!

- Provide special support for ELL families. Classroom volunteers can record texts in English for children to take home. Together, the parent and child can listen to the recording (several times, if necessary) and then read aloud along with the taped version. Tuck some vocabulary practice into these lessons by using one of the activities in Chapter 2, such as "Word Pyramids" or "Word Spokes." Even better, use the resources in Chapter 5 to generate a word search or crossword puzzle with words from the text. These playful activities will deliver oral and written language practice that children will find irresistible.

Reflection Protocol

Book Club

ACED: Analysis, Clarification, Extension, Discussion

I. REFLECTION (10 to 15 minutes)

ANALYSIS:

- What, for you, were the most interesting and/or important ideas in this chapter?

  _____

  _____

  _____

  _____

- What information was new to you?

  _____

  _____

  _____

  _____

CLARIFICATION:

- Did anything surprise you? Confuse you?

  _____

  _____

  _____

  _____

EXTENSION:

- What questions do you have?

  _____

  _____

  _____

  _____

II. DISCUSSION (30 minutes)

- Form groups of 4 to 6 members.
- Appoint a *facilitator (timer)* and *recorder.*
- Share responses. Make sure that each person has shared his or her responses to each category (Analysis/Clarification/Extension).
- Help each other with any areas of confusion.
- Answer and/or discuss questions raised by group members.
- On chart paper, the recorder should summarize the main discussion points and identify issues or questions the group would like to raise for general discussion.

III. APPLICATION (10 minutes)

- Based on your reflection and discussion, how might you apply what you have learned from this chapter?

_____

_____

_____

_____

_____

Reflection

1. What key math, social studies, and science concepts are children expected to learn in your classroom? For each content area, make a list of the key concepts and then list ways (e.g., language experience, word banks, literature, writing) that you can help children learn the vocabulary words essential to understanding these concepts.

   _____

   _____

   _____

   _____

2. Work with a colleague who also teaches at your grade level. Discuss these issues and make notes about your answers. How much vocabulary instruction should be whole-group oriented? How much should be small-group oriented? What kinds of groups should be formed? How much individual work should be assigned? And for all of these questions, why? After your discussion, share your ideas with others in your professional development group.

   _____

   _____

   _____

   _____

3. Work with a colleague to identify specific activities you can use to simultaneously meet the needs of children who are (a) "struggling" readers and/or writers; (b) "advanced" readers and/or writers; and (c) learning English as a second language. How might you differentiate instruction for each of these student populations in a way that is both time efficient for lesson planning and easily integrated into instructional routines? After your discussion, share your ideas with others in your professional development group.

   _____

   _____

   _____

   _____

4. In the Principals' FAQ Project (Mraz et al., 2001) principals provided questions about vocabulary that parents frequently asked. Two questions are listed here. Work in a small group comprised of both veteran and novice teachers. Use what you have learned through this professional development program to compile responses to each question.

- What are context clues?

  _____

  _____

  _____

- When should I stop reading aloud to my child?

  _____

  _____

  _____

  For additional questions and answers, go to www.educ.kent .edu/TLCS/centers/RWD/qa.htm.

5. Work with a small group (two or three other teachers). Read the following vignette and discuss the questions. Then share your ideas and insights with others in your professional development group.

Book Club

VIGNETTE

Carla's parents are migrant workers. Soon Carla will come to your first-grade class for three months before she and her family move on. Carla attended your school's kindergarten for three months as well. Your kindergarten colleague reports that Carla was curious and active but she seemed to have difficulty picking up English vocabulary.

Carla spends her first week in your classroom drawing pictures of and writing about her family. Although you can't read her writing, you suspect that she is inventing spelling in Spanish. She looks at you when you speak to her and appears to pay attention during class discussions and read-alouds. On the few occasions when she speaks, she often says only "yes," "no," or "OK."

- What do you think Carla knows about English vocabulary? How can you find out about her conversational fluency in English? About her knowledge of the language of schooling?

  _____

  _____

  _____

- What instructional goals related to vocabulary learning seem appropriate for Carla? What activities? How will you assess her progress toward the goals?

  _____

  _____

  _____

6. What do parents need to know about vocabulary? How can this information be communicated?

  _____

  _____

  _____

7. Complete one or both of the following charts with your insights and plans for vocabulary instruction.

Curriculum Alignment

Component	What Is...	What Should Be...
Curriculum		
Instruction		
Materials		
Assessment		
Home Connection		

Source: Adapted from Taylor and Collins (2003).

Goal Planning

Goal _____

Plans by_____ Date _____

Action Steps: What do I need to do?	Materials/Resources	Evaluation: How will I assess the usefulness of this change?

CHAPTER 5

Resources

*I*n this final chapter, we offer resources for classroom activities and for your own further learning. Both print and Web-based resources are provided.

Websites

Websites for Word Play (for students)

Learning Vocabulary Can Be Fun! www.vocabulary.co.il/

There is something here for all age and skill levels. Students can play "Match Game" and "Hangman" or do crossword puzzles, word searches, and jumbles. All the activities are for one player.

Vocabulary Builders (Grades 3–5)
www.manatee.k12.fl.us/sites/elementary/palmasola/rvocabindex.htm

Full of electronic activities students can do themselves and practice sheets you can duplicate. Includes activities on prefixes, suffixes, antonyms, synonyms, homophones, multiple meanings, context, and more. An online student dictionary kids will enjoy!

Vocabulary University www.vocabulary.com/

Full of puzzles and other activities based on Greek and Latin roots. The puzzles change regularly, so students can visit the site frequently without getting bored!

Explore English Words from Greek-Latin Origins
www.wordexplorations.com/

Lots of references and interesting resources! Students will enjoy *"Words for Our Modern Age: Especially English Words from Greek and Latin Sources."*

Word Games and Puzzles! http://mindfun.com/

Calls itself the "web's best spot for online trivia games, word puzzles and quizzes!" Students will find word scrambles, webs, crossword puzzles—even Boggle! Lots of word trivia too!

Word Central www.wordcentral.com/

Sponsored by Barnes & Noble, this site has plenty of activities and information for students, as well as resources (including lesson plans) for teachers. You can even build your own dictionary!!

Surfing the Net with Kids www.surfnetkids.com/games/

Lots of free kids' games listed by type (e.g., crossword, jigsaw), topic (e.g., science, geography), or theme (e.g., sports, dress-up, holidays). The site also has an easy-to-use search tool.

Interactive Wordplays www.wordplays.com

> Full of word games (e.g., anagrams, jumbles, crossword puzzles) that can even be played in several different languages. A multilingual dictionary is also available here.

Websites for Word Roots/Word Lists (for teachers)

Building Vocabulary

> www.learner.org/jnorth/tm/tips/Tip0023.html#Families
>
> Sponsored by "Journey North," this site has quick and easy vocabulary activities you can do in your classroom.

Lists of Latin and Greek Roots

> www.awrsd.org/oak/Library/greek_and_latin_root_words.htm
> www.factmonster.com/ipka/A0907017.html
> academic.cuesta.edu/acasupp/as/506.htm

Word Roots and Prefixes www.virtualsalt.com/roots.htm

> Has lists of roots and words that come from them.

Most Frequently Used Words Lists www.esldesk.com/esl-quizzes/frequently-used-english-words/words.htm

> This useful site will take you, in increments of 300, to the 1,000 most frequently used words in the English language.

Websites to Make Your Own Word Games! (for teachers)

Instant Online Crossword Puzzlemaker www.varietygames.com/CW/

> Make your own crossword puzzle in a flash! Then print for your students to enjoy! You can make the puzzles simple or complicated, so this site is good for teachers working at all levels!

Word Search www.armoredpenguin.com/wordsearch/

> This site has a "generator" that will create your own word jumbles and puzzles!

FunBrain Word Turtle www.funbrain.com/detect/

> You or your students can give "Fun Brain" a list of words that it will hide in a puzzle. Students can choose skill level and play alone or with a friend. They can also play ready-made puzzles based on some favorite children's literature. Make your own puzzles for them to play!

Superkids Wordsearch Puzzle

www.superkids.com/aweb/tools/words/search/

Make your own printable hidden word puzzles using the SuperKids Word-search Puzzle Creator. Kids will love solving these word searches that take you only a few minutes to make up!

Discovery School's Word Search Puzzlemaker

http://puzzlemaker.school.discovery.com/WordSearchSetupForm.html

Another wordsearch generator! This one gives more options for letter use and word type.

Electronic Dictionaries and References (for teachers and students)

The Big List www.wordorigins.org/

This site explains the origin of over 400 familiar words and phrases, selected because they are "interesting or because some bit of folklore, sometimes true and sometimes false, is associated with the origin." Dazzle students with your own knowledge or let them explore for themselves!

Allwords.com www.allwords.com/

Has an online dictionary that does a multilingual search that children who are learning English as a second language will find very useful. "Links for Word Lovers" will take you to all kinds of resources for information (dictionaries, thesaurus, etymologies) and word play (puns, rhymes, songs, quotations).

One Look Dictionary Search www.onelook.com/

Type in a word and let this site look it up in several dictionaries! It also has a "Reverse Dictionary": You type in a description of the concept and it finds words and phrases that match it.

Little Explorers English Picture Dictionary

www.enchantedlearning.com/Dictionary.html

Click on a letter of the alphabet and your students will find dozens of words that begin with that letter. Each of the 2,472 words has a picture and a defini-tion. Best of all, this site also has picture dictionaries that go from English to Spanish, French, Italian, Portugese, German, Swedish, Dutch, and Japanese! These dictionaries will captivate all your students and provide extra support to English language learners.

Online Etymology Dictionary www.wordexplorations.com/

Type in a word — any word — and this dictionary will tell you its history! This one is fun for you and your students!

Thesaurus.com thesaurus.reference.com/

Type in a word and quickly find synonyms and antonyms for it. This site also has a dictionary, an encyclopedia, and a word-of-the-day in English and Spanish.

Websites for Further Professional Reading

- "A Focus on Vocabulary" from Pacific Resources for Education and Learning provides an excellent overview of vocabulary research with in-depth information in a reader-friendly format. This downloadable booklet (44 pages) from the *Research-Based Practices in Early Reading* series could be used for additional professional development or even shared with parents. (Go to http://eric.ed.gov/ERIC and search for file ED483190.)

- The chapter "Building a Robust Vocabulary," from Linda Hoyt's book *Spotlight on Comprehension* (Heinemann, 2003), can be downloaded directly from Hoyt's website (www.lindahoyt.com/ Products/products.htm). The chapter provides classroom examples of good vocabulary instruction for the primary grades. There are also a few activity sheets you can use with your students at the end of the chapter.

- For a research-based analysis of the diversity of word learning styles, read "Vocabulary Acquisition: Synthesis of the Research," by Baker, Simmons, and Kameenui. The document, funded by the U.S. Office of Special Education Programs, can be found at the National Center to Improve the Tools of Educators website (idea.uoregon.edu/~ncite/documents.html). Look for it under "Technical Reports of Reading Research Synthesis."

- If you are interested in more ideas about how students can use the Web for vocabulary growth, read Karen Bromley's "Vocabulary Learning Online." It can be found at Reading Online (www.readingonline.org/), an electronic journal of the International Reading Association.

- Also available at Reading Online (www.readingonline.org/) is Tim Rasinski's "Making and Writing Words," a popular word study activity. You will find detailed planning instructions, classroom examples, blackline masters, and a discussion forum where you can share tips with other teachers.

- Although there are few websites that support the vocabulary development of elementary-aged English language learners, go to "everything ESL.net" (www.everythingesl.net/inservices/ elementary_sites_ells_71638.php) for links to dozens of sites (identified according to grade levels) having enjoyable and beneficial activities for English language learners.

Teacher Resource Books and Articles

Classroom Activities

Blachowicz, C., & Fisher, P. J. (2006). *Teaching vocabulary in all classrooms* (3rd ed.). Upper Saddle River, NJ: Merrill/Prentice-Hall.

> Each chapter is full of classroom-tested strategies. Topics include content area vocabulary, integrating reading and writing, learning from context, using reference sources, word play, and assessment.

Brassell, D., & Flood, J. (2004). *Vocabulary strategies every teacher needs to know.* San Diego, CA: Academic Professional Development.

> Twenty-five strategies, some familiar and some new, with easy-to-follow instructions and easy-to-duplicate templates.

Fitzgerald, J., & Graves, M. (2004). *Scaffolding reading experiences for English-language learners.* Norwood, MA: Christopher Gordon.

> Although the focus of this text is on teaching reading to second language learners, there are excellent suggestions for how to introduce these children to new vocabulary.

Hoyt, L. (1999). *Revisit, reflect, retell: Strategies for improving reading comprehension.* Portsmouth, NH: Heinemann.

> Strategies for supporting comprehension development, including through vocabulary. Activities are presented in easy-to-use, student-friendly formats.

Morris, A. (2005). *Vocabulary unplugged: 30 lessons that will revolutionize how you teach vocabulary K–12.* Shoreham, VT: Discover Writing Press.

> The title says it all. Many activities students will enjoy presented in an easy-to-follow lesson plan format.

Nickelsen, L. (1998). *Quick activities to build a very voluminous vocabulary.* New York: Scholastic.

> Fifty easy-to-implement activities that can be adapted for most grade levels.

Rasinski, T. (2001). *Making and writing words (Grades 3–6).* Greensboro, NC: Carson-Dellosa Publishing.

> Lots of ready-to-use activities.

Rasinski, T. (2005). *Daily word ladders (Grades 2–3).* New York: Scholastic.

> Children will enjoy the challenge of "climbing" these 100 developmentally appropriate (and easily duplicated) "ladders."

Rasinski, T., Padak, N., Newton, R., & Newton, E. (2007). *Building vocabulary from word roots (Level 3).* Huntington Beach, CA: Teacher Created Materials/(Beach City Press).

> Introduces a new root each week, with daily guided practice activities. (Set includes teachers' manual with overheads and full-color workbooks for students.)

For Further Reading

Beck, I. L., McKeown, M. G., & Kucan, L. (2002). *Bringing words to life: Robust vocabulary instruction.* New York: Guilford.

Explains a three-tier system for choosing and teaching vocabulary for reading comprehension.

Brand, M. (2004). *Word savvy: Integrated vocabulary, spelling, & word study, grades 3–6.* Portland, MA: Stenhouse.

An Ohio teacher describes how he weaves word study throughout the day. Provides advice and many specific examples that are easily adaptable to the primary grades.

Fry, E. B. (2004). *The vocabulary teacher's book of lists.* San Francisco, CA: Jossey-Bass.

Lists of words from content subjects such as math and science to word study with prefixes, roots, homophones, and more.

Paynter, D., Bodrova, E., & Doty, J. K. (2005). *For the love of words: Vocabulary instruction that works.* San Francisco, CA: Jossey-Bass.

Practical ideas for expanding the role of vocabulary in reading, writing, and thinking.

Rasinski, T. V., & Padak, N. (2004). *Effective reading strategies: Teaching children who find reading difficult* (3rd ed.). Columbus, OH: Merrill/Prentice Hall.

Identifies strategies that target specific needs, including vocabulary and word study, of children who can use extra support in learning to read.

Stahl, S. (1999). *Vocabulary development.* Cambridge, MA: Brookline.

From the *Reading Research to Practice* series for teachers, this short book gives an overview of the most important principles to think about when planning vocabulary instruction. It also gives valuable background information about the relationship between vocabulary and comprehension.

Children's Books for Word Play

Cleary, B. P. (1999). *A mink, a fink, a skating rink: What is a noun?* Minneapolis, MN: Carolrhoda.

Cleary, B. P. (2001). *To root, to toot, to parachute: What is a verb?* Minneapolis, MN: Carolrhoda.

Cleary, B. P. (2004). *Pitch and throw, grasp and know: What is a synonym?* Minneapolis, MN: Carolrhoda.

Cleary, B. P. (2006). *Stop and go, yes and no: What is an antonym?* Minneapolis, MN: Millbrook.

Frasier, D. (2000). *Miss Alaineus: A vocabulary disaster.* San Diego, CA: Harcourt.

Gwynne, F. (1976). *A chocolate moose for dinner.* New York: Aladdin.

Gwynne, F. (1987, 2006). *The king who rained.* New York: Aladdin.

Parish, P., & Parish, H. *Amelia Bedelia* series. New York: HarperCollins.

Terban, M. (1982). *Eight ate: A feast of homonym riddles.* New York: Clarion.

Terban, M. (1996). *Dictionary of idioms.* New York: Scholastic.

Children's Dictionary Books

Merriam Webster Children's Dictionary. (2005). DK Publishing. For ages 4–8.

My First Dictionary. (1993). DK Children. For ages 4–8.

DK Children's Illustrated Dictionary. (1994). DK Children. For ages 4–8.

Scholastic Children's Dictionary. (2002). Scholastic. For ages 4–8.

More Vocabulary Development Resources

Primary/Elementary Level Word Roots

(Order of roots is not sequential.)

Prefixes

co-, con-	with, together
de-	down, off of
ex-	out
in-	not *("negative")*
pre-	before
re-	back, again
sub-	under, below
un-	not *("negative")*

Bases

audi-, audit-	hear, listen
graph-, gram-	write, draw
mov-, mot-, mobil-	move
port-	carry
vid-, vis-	see

Numerical Bases (appear at beginning of words)

uni-, unit-	one
bi-	two
tri-	three
quart-, quadr-	four, fourth
quint-	five, fifth
sext-, hex-	six, sixth
sept-, hept-	seven, seventh
oct-	eight, eighth
dec-, deci(m)-,	ten, tenth
cent-	one hundred
mill-	one thousand
semi-, hemi-	one half
equ(i)-	equal

Suffixes

-able, -ible	can, able to be done
-er,	more
-est	most
-ful	full of
-less	without

Divide and Conquer These Words!

	Prefix	+	Base	Word Means
1.	_____	_____	_____	_____
2.	_____	_____	_____	_____
3.	_____	_____	_____	_____
4.	_____	_____	_____	_____
5.	_____	_____	_____	_____
6.	_____	_____	_____	_____
7.	_____	_____	_____	_____
8.	_____	_____	_____	_____
9.	_____	_____	_____	_____
10.	_____	_____	_____	_____

Look over the words in "Divide and Conquer." Then answer these questions:

1. Choose a word whose meaning you already knew. Write the word. What does it mean?

_____   _____

_____

2. Choose a word you find very interesting that you did not know before. Write the word. What does it mean? Why do you find it interesting?

_____   _____

_____

3. Choose a new word you think is very hard. Write the word. What does it mean? Tell why you think it is hard.

_____   _____

_____

Source: Rusinski, Padak, Newton, and Newton (2007).

CLUE: Circle-Look-Underline-Explain

Circle a word you don't know in each sentence. *Look* at the words around it. *Underline* any words that give you clues about its meaning. *Explain* what you think the word might mean. How did the context clue words help?

1._____

_____

Explain _____

_____

_____

2._____

_____

Explain _____

_____

_____

3._____

_____

Explain _____

_____

_____

4._____

_____

Explain _____

_____

_____

Word Mapping

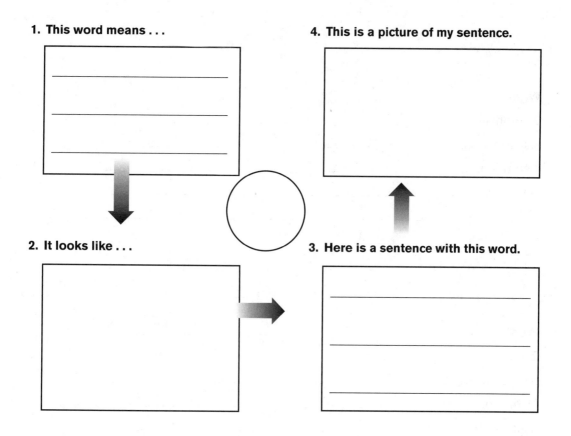

1. **This word means . . .**

2. **It looks like . . .**

4. **This is a picture of my sentence.**

3. **Here is a sentence with this word.**

Word Pyramids

Work with a partner to make word pyramids.

Word: _____

2 antonyms: _____   _____

3 synonyms: _____   _____   _____

Definition: _____   _____   _____   _____

Sentence: _____

_____

Word: _____

2 antonyms: _____   _____

3 synonyms: _____   _____   _____

Definition: _____   _____   _____   _____

Sentence: _____

_____

Word Spokes

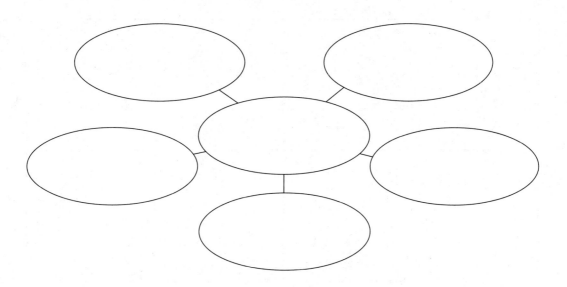

Choose a different word from your cluster for each of the following directions.

1. Pick one of the words and write **2 synonyms.**

Word _____ 1. _____ 2. _____

2. Pick one of the words and write **2 antonyms.**

Word _____ 1. _____ 2. _____

3. Pick one of the words and **write your own definition.**

_____

4. Pick one of the words and **use it in a sentence.**

_____

5. Take the last word and do any **one** of the activities in 1–4.

_____

_____

Source: Rasinski, Padak, Newton, and Newton (2007).

Wordo

Source: Rasinski, Padak, Newton, and Newton (2007).

Scattergories

CATEGORIES				
Initial Consonants & Blends ⬇				

Alphaboxes

A	B	C	D
E	F	G	H
I	J	K	L
M	N	O	P
Q	R	S	T
U	V	W	XYZ

Words Knew and New

Read the story. Then go back and answer these questions.

1. Pick out a word whose meaning you already knew. Write the word.
   What does it mean?

   _____

   _____

   _____

2. Pick out a word you find very interesting that you did not know
   before. Write the word. What does it mean? Why do you find it interesting?

   _____

   _____

   _____

3. Pick out a new word you think is very hard. Write the word. What
   do you think it means? Tell why you think it is hard. How did you
   figure it out?

   _____

   _____

   _____

4. Write one sentence with two of the three words you chose.

   _____

   _____

   _____

5. Now write one sentence with the remaining word.

   _____

   _____

   _____

APPENDIX B

Book Club Ideas

*T*hroughout the book, you have seen icons indicating activities or discussion points that lend themselves to book club conversations. We hope you and your colleagues will take advantage of these opportunities. Our experience has taught us that learning from and with each other is a powerful way to promote innovation. In this appendix, we provide additional questions and ideas for discussion. They are organized according to the chapters in the book.

Introduction: Vocabulary

- Look more closely at the vocabulary chapter in the report of the National Reading Panel. Make notes about key insights and the classroom implications of these insights. Share these with colleagues. (The report is available at www.nationalreading panel.org. A shorter version of the report is available at www.nifl.gov/partnershipforreading/publications/PFRbooklet BW.pdf.)

- Select a piece of follow-up reading from the NRP web site or at the National Institute for Literacy (http://nifl.gov). Make notes and share these with your colleagues.

- Think back to the beginning of your teaching career. What were you taught about teaching vocabulary? Share these insights with colleagues and together attempt to determine how vocabulary instruction has changed over time. What has been the role of mass communication media and other technological advances on vocabulary teaching and learning?

Chapter 1: Vocabulary: What Does Research Tell Us?

Book Club

- Make notes about the relationship between vocabulary and reading achievement. With your colleagues, write a paragraph that explains this relationship.
- Talk with colleagues about why some children may have difficulty learning new vocabulary. For each reason you can identify, make instructional plans for addressing it.
- Talk with colleagues about how you can draw attention to vocabulary during teacher read-alouds.
- Brainstorm with colleagues ways in which you can increase your emphasis on vocabulary instruction throughout the school day. Focus on ways to stimulate students' curiosity about words. Make concrete plans for integrating these ideas into your instructional routines.
- Brainstorm ways you can share your own love of words with your students. Make concrete plans for integrating these ideas into your instructional routines.

Chapter 2: Instructional Strategies for Vocabulary Development

- Decide on the two or three instructional activities best suited for your classroom. Explain to your colleagues why each activity is a good fit.
- For each activity selected, make plans for implementation. Keep track of questions. Share your plans with colleagues and discuss the questions.
- For each activity selected, make plans to assess impact. That is, how will you determine if these new activities are enhancing your students' vocabulary? Share your ideas with colleagues and invite them to offer feedback.
- If you are currently using a basal reading series or a commercial vocabulary program, evaluate it using the questions posed at the end of the chapter. If your evaluation identifies weaknesses, discuss these with your colleagues. Make plans to strengthen these weak areas if possible.

Chapter 3: Assessing Vocabulary Development

- Discuss each "big idea" about assessment in more detail. Decide if you agree or disagree with each, why, and what implications the ideas have for your classroom assessment plans for vocabulary.

- List all possible revisions to your classroom assessment plans for vocabulary. Then rank-order these. Explain your reasoning to your colleagues.

- For the most important revision idea from the activity above, develop an implementation plan. Share this with your colleagues and seek their feedback.

Chapter 4: Beyond Strategies

- Develop detailed notes about the following: How will you explain vocabulary development to parents? How will you help parents see the role they play in promoting their children's vocabulary development?

- Review the chapter's suggested activities for supporting a child's vocabulary development at home. Select those activities that you believe would be useful and feasible for the families of your students. Make detailed plans for sharing the activities you selected with these families.

- Brainstorm ways in which children who speak a language other than English can enhance the vocabulary learning experiences of all your students. What unique contributions can they make based on their cultural and linguistic backgrounds? Make concrete plans for integrating these ideas into your instructional routines.

Chapter 5: Resources

- Review the list of websites for word play. Select two or more sites that you do not currently use with your students. Make plans for incorporating these sites in your instructional plans. Describe the sites and explain your plans to colleagues.

- Review the list of websites for word roots, word lists, and generating your own word games. Select two or more sites that have resources you can use to plan instruction. Describe the sites and tell your colleagues how you will use them.

- Review the list of websites for electronic dictionaries and references. Select two or more of these sites that you can use with students or to plan instruction. Describe the sites and tell your colleagues how you will use them.

- Review the list of Websites for Further Professional Readings. Decide on one article for the whole group to read and discuss together. Before you begin reading, use the strategy of "Word Predictions" (see Chapter 2) to activate background knowledge.

- Review the list of books that engage children in word play. Discuss with colleagues other useful sources that you could add to this list. Discuss suggestions for ways in which these sources can be used with students.

- Search the Web for additional resources and sites that can provide support for vocabulary instruction. Share these with your colleagues.

Appendix C

Notes

*A*s you work through the book, you may want to make notes here about important ideas gleaned from discussions. You can keep track of additional resources. You may also want to use these pages to reflect on changes you made in your vocabulary instruction and to make notes about next steps.

General Issues and Ideas

_____

_____

_____

_____

_____

_____

_____

_____

_____

_____

_____

_____

_____

_____

_____

_____

_____

Instructional Plans

Assessment Plans

Resources for Teachers

References

Ayers, D. M. (1986). *English words from Latin and Greek elements* (2nd ed.). Tucson, AZ: University of Arizona Press.

Barger, J. (2006). Teaching tips: Building word consciousness. *The Reading Teacher, 60,* 279–281.

Baumann, J. F., & Kameenui, E. J. (2004). *Vocabulary instruction: Research to practice.* New York: Guilford.

Beck, I. L., McKeown, M. G., & Kucan, L. (2002). *Bringing words to life: Robust vocabulary instruction.* New York: Guilford.

Biemiller, A. (2001). Teaching vocabulary: Early, direct, and sequential. *American Educator, 25*(1), 24–28.

Biemiller, A. (2005). Size and sequence in vocabulary development: Implications for choosing words for primary grade vocabulary. In E. H. Hiebert & M. L. Kamil (Eds.), *Teaching and learning vocabulary: Bringing research to practice* (pp. 223–242). Mahwah, NJ: Erlbaum.

Blachowicz, C. L. Z., & Fisher, P. (2000). Vocabulary instruction. In M. L. Kamil, P. B. Mosenthal, P. D. Pearson, & R. Barr (Eds.), *Handbook of reading research, volume III* (pp. 503–523). White Plains, NY: Longman.

Blachowicz, C. L. Z., & Fisher, P. (2004). Vocabulary lessons. *Educational Leadership, 61*(6), 66–69.

Blachowicz, C. L. Z. & Fisher, P. (2006). *Teaching vocabulary in all classrooms* (3rd ed.). Upper Saddle River, NJ: Pearson/Merrill/Prentice Hall.

Brand, M. (2004). *Word savvy: Integrated vocabulary, spelling, & word study, grades 3–6.* Portland, MA: Stenhouse.

Burgess, S. R. (1999). The influence of speech perception, oral language ability, the home literacy environment, and prereading knowledge on the growth of phonological sensitivity: A 1-year longitudinal study. *Reading Research Quarterly, 34,* 400–402.

Cooter, R., Marrin, P., & Mills-House, E. (1999). Family and community involvement: The bedrock of reading success. *The Reading Teacher, 52,* 891–896.

Daniels, H. (2002). *Literature circles: Voice and choice in book clubs and reading groups.* Portland, ME: Stenhouse.

Darling-Hammond, L., & McLaughlin, M. W. (1995). Policies that support professional development in an era of reform. *Phi Delta Kappan, 76,* 597–604.

Fitzgerald J., & Graves, M. (2004). *Scaffolding reading experiences for English-language learners.* Norwood, MA: Christopher Gordon.

Fry, E. B. (2004). *The vocabulary teacher's book of lists.* San Francisco: Jossey-Bass.

Harris, T. L., & Hodges, R. E. (Eds.). (1995). *The literacy dictionary: The vocabulary of reading and writing.* Newark, DE: International Reading Association.

Hart, B., & Risley, T. R. (1995). *Meaningful differences in the everyday experience of young American children.* Baltimore: Brookes.

Hoyt, L. (1999). *Revisit, reflect, retell: Strategies for improving reading comprehension.* Portsmouth, NH: Heinemann.

Kamil, M. L., & Hiebert, E. H. (2005). Teaching and learning vocabulary: Perspectives and persistent issues. In E. H. Hiebert & M. L. Kamil (Eds.), *Teaching and learning vocabulary: Bringing research to practice* (pp. 1–23). Mahwah, NJ: Erlbaum.

Lehr, F., Osborn, J., & Hiebert, E. H. (2004). *Research-based practices in early reading series: A focus on vocabulary.* Retrieved January 15, 2007, from www.prel.org/products/re_/ES0419.htm.

McTighe, J., & Wiggins, G. (2004). *Understanding by design.* Alexandria, VA: Association for Supervision and Curriculum Development.

Morris, A. (2005). *Vocabulary unplugged: 30 lessons that will revolutionize how you teach vocabulary K–12.* Shoreham VT: Discover Writing Press.

Mraz, M., Gruhler, D., Padak, N., Peck, J., Kinner, J., McKeon, C., & Newton, E. (2001). Questions parents ask: The FAQ project. In W. Linek, E. Sturtevant, J. Dugan, & P. Linder (Eds.), *Celebrating the voices of literacy* (pp. 252–262). Readyville, TN: College Reading Association.

Nagy, W. E., & Anderson, R. C. (1984). How many words are there in printed school English? *Reading Research Quarterly, 19,* 304–330.

Nagy, W. E., Anderson, R. C., Schommer, M., Scott, J. A., & Stallman, A. (1989). Morphological families in the internal lexicon. *Reading Research Quarterly, 24,* 262–282.

Nagy, W. E., & Herman, P. A. (1987). Depth and breadth of vocabulary knowledge: Implications for acquisition and instruction. In M. G. McKeown & M. E. Curtis (Eds.), *The nature of vocabulary acquisition* (pp. 24–56). Hillsdale, NJ: Erlbaum.

National Reading Panel. (2000). *Teaching children to read: An evidence-based assessment of the scientific research literature in reading and its implications for reading instruction.* Washington, DC: National Institute of Child Health & Human Development.

Newton, R. M., & Newton, E. (2005). A little Latin and a lot of English. *Adolescent literacy in perspective.* Retrieved December 15, 2006, from The Ohio Resource Center for Mathematics, Science and Reading, www.ohiorc.org.

Nickelsen, L. (1998). *Quick activities to build a very voluminous vocabulary.* New York: Scholastic.

Paynter, D., Bodrova, E., & Doty, J. K. (2005). *For the love of words: Vocabulary instruction that works.* San Francisco: Jossey-Bass.

Rasinski, T. (2001). *Making and writing words (grades 3–6).* Greensboro, NC: Carson-Dellosa Publishing.

Rasinski, T. (2005). *Daily word ladders (grades 2–3).* New York: Scholastic.

Rasinski, T., & Padak, N. (2004). *Effective reading strategies: Teaching children who find reading difficult* (3rd ed.). Upper Saddle River, NJ: Pearson.

Rasinski, T., Padak, N., Newton, R., & Newton, E. (2007). *Building vocabulary from word roots (Level 3).* Huntington Beach, CA: Teacher Created Materials (Beach City Press).

Renyi, J. (1998). Building learning into the teaching job. *Educational Leadership, 55*(5), 70–74.

Senechal, M., LeFevre, J., & Thomas, E. (1998). Differential effects of home literacy experiences on the development of oral and written language. *Reading Research Quarterly, 33,* 96–116.

Simpson, J., & Weiner, E. (Eds.). (2006). *The Oxford English dictionary.* New York: Oxford University Press.

Stahl, S. (1999). *Vocabulary development.* Cambridge, MA: Brookline.

Stahl, S. A., & Fairbanks, M. M. (1986). The effects of vocabulary instruction: A model-based meta-analysis. *Review of Educational Research, 56*(1), 72–110.

Tierney, R. (1998). Literacy assessment reform: Shifting beliefs, principled possibilities, and emerging practices. *The Reading Teacher, 51,* 374–390.

Wenglinsky, H. (2000). *How teaching matters: Bringing the classroom back into discussions of teacher quality.* Princeton, NJ: Educational Testing Service.

West, K. (1998). Noticing and responding to learners: Literacy evaluation and instruction in the primary grades. *The Reading Teacher, 51,* 550–559.

White, T. G., Sowell, J., & Yanagihara, A. (1989). Teaching elementary students to use word-part clues. *The Reading Teacher, 42,* 302–309.

Children's Literature

Carle, E. (1995). *Walter the baker.* New York: Simon & Schuster.

Cowley, J. (1990). *Mrs. Wishy-Washy.* DeSoto, TX: Wright Group.

Fox, Mem. (1989). *Koala Lou.* San Diego, CA: Gulliver's Books (Harcourt).

Parish, P. (1995). *Amelia Bedelia's treasury.* New York: HarperCollins Childrens.